BUSINESS ENGLISH WRITING: ADVANCED MASTERCLASS

HOW TO COMMUNICATE EFFECTIVELY & COMMUNICATE WITH CONFIDENCE: HOW TO WRITE EMAILS, BUSINESS LETTERS & BUSINESS REPORTS

INCLUDES 100 + BUSINESS LETTER TEMPLATES & BUSINESS EMAILS

Macson Bell Coaching & Training ®

www.macsonbell.com

Contents

Business writing is the art of painting pictures with words, the science of turning data into narratives, and the diplomacy of inspiring action through communication. It is the silent ambassador of your professional credibility.

Foreword

In the midst of the hustle and bustle of modern business, it is the ability to communicate effectively that sets you apart from everyone else. Over the last decade, I've had the extraordinary privilege of guiding hundreds of professionals on their journey to business writing mastery, report writing, proposal writing, and data presentation. It's a true honour to have been able to help so many outstanding people.

The information in this book comes from hundreds of hours of research, thousands of hours of teaching and coaching, and from the thousands of emails, reports, memos, proposals, and books I've written and coached clients on.

I hope this resource can serve as your compass, guiding you towards becoming a more confident, persuasive, and effective communicator in the world of work. Your journey to mastering Business English Writing begins here.

Enjoy the ride.

Best Regards,

Marc

About This Business English Book

Master Business Communication with *'Business English Writing: Advanced Masterclass'*

'Business English Writing: Advanced Masterclass' is an all-encompassing self-study guide, designed for those who want to communicate effectively and with confidence. This book is your key to unlocking the world of professional communication, helping you to write about data, and produce compelling business letters, professional emails, and reports.

The *Masterclass* takes a unique, step-by-step approach to each task, making it ideal for both beginners and experienced learners seeking to enhance their Business English skills. This book provides real-world applicability, ensuring that learners are primed to perform at their best in any professional scenario.

One of the standout features of this business writing book is its focus on building confidence. With each unit, learners will find themselves more comfortable in creating fluent and advanced business documents. The specialized business grammar exercises interspersed in each unit act as a guide, showing learners how to seamlessly incorporate various grammatical elements into their writing.

Chapter 1: Decoding and Describing Graph Data

Visual data representation, is an integral part of business communication. The power of a graph lies not just in its ability to visually represent trends and changes but also in the efficacy of the language used to interpret and describe it. Consequently, this first chapter will focus on using the power of language to describe changes in graph data effectively.

We will start this journey by expanding your vocabulary and improving your understanding of grammar structures typically used for describing changes. The nuances of the English language will be explored, as we dive into a toolbox of words and phrases that you can use to write (or speak) about trends, fluctuations, increases, and decreases. This toolkit of language resources will empower you to interpret graph data accurately and communicate your insights with precision.

As we progress through this chapter, we'll learn how to craft compelling narratives from graph data, allowing you to turn raw data into insightful stories. Whether you're analyzing a sales graph, presenting market trends, or forecasting future projections, the skills you practice in this chapter will enable you to communicate your findings with confidence and clarity.

Welcome to Chapter 1.

Exercise 1

Match the words of change with the parts of the graph. More than one option is possible.

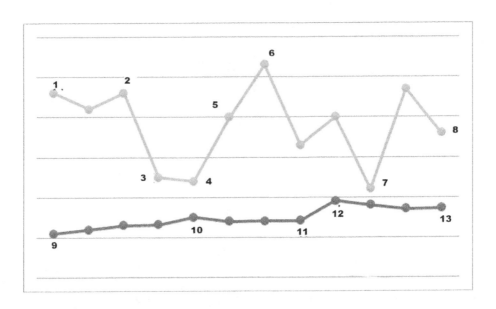

1-2 ....

2-3 ....

2-4 ....

4-6 ....

6 ....

6-8 ....

7 ....

9-10 ....

10-11 ....

12-13 ....

Rose *steadily* or *increased steadily*	Rose *dramatically* or *increased dramatically*	Rose *gradually* or *increased gradually*
Plummeted to or *Plunged to* ...	*Hit a peak of,* or *Peaked at,* or *reached a high of* ...	*Fluctuated, varied,* or *oscillated*
Dropped/ Shrank/ Fell drastically/ sharply dramatically	*Remained flat/ unchanged/ stable / constant at*	*Dropped and then levelled off/ evened out at*
Hit a low of .../ *bottomed out at*	*Dropped and then quickly recovered*	*Dipped / Declined slightly before quickly recovering*
Rocketed / Soared	*Fell slowly/ gradually / steadily*	*Was erratic/ inconsistent*

Definitions for some words

Word	Explanation
Dipped	Fell slightly but recovered quickly
Bottomed out / Hit a low of	The lowest point on the graph
Plummeted to.../ Plunged to	Suffered a quick and drastic or shocking decrease. Fell extremely quickly. A very quick and large drop or reduction
Fluctuated/ was erratic	Increases and decreases randomly, irregularly or unpredictably
Rose/increased dramatically/ Soared/ Rocketed	Increased very quickly and drastically
Peaked at / reached a high of	The highest point on the graph
Remained constant/unchanged/stable at ..../ Levelled off/evened out at ...	a part of the graph where there is no change

Answers

1-2 *Fell and then quickly recovered / Dipped/ fell slightly*

2-3 *Fell/ dropped/ shrank drastically/ dramatically / sharply/ Plummeted to/ Plunged to*

2-4 *Dropped and then levelled off/ evened out at*

4-6 *Rose/ increased dramatically/ Soared/ Rocketed*

6 *Hit a peak / Peaked at/ reached a high of*

6-8 *Fluctuated/ was erratic*

7 *Hit a low of …*

9-10 *Rose/ increased steadily/ Rose/ increased gradually*

10-11 *Remained flat/ constant/ unchanged/ stable at*

12-13 *Fell gradually / steadily*

Please note that these are only some of the options from the table.

Mastering Sentence Structures to Describe Change

Take a look at the following graph and read the paragraph which describes it.

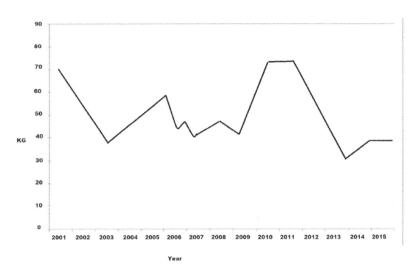

Average Kg of rice per household per year

Graph Description:

Initially, in 2001, the average number of kg of rice consumed per household per year was 70, but over the next four years, there was a dramatic drop to 35 kg per year (annum). The number then increased (grew, rose, climbed) significantly between 2005 and 2006 to 60 kg per year (per annum). 2006 to 2009 saw an erratic period (a fluctuation) in the amount of rice consumed, which was followed by a sharp rise at the end of the period, with the figures hitting a peak (an all-time high) of 75 Kg in 2010. It levelled off for the next year, but then the average consumption plummeted, hitting a low (an all-time low) of 30 Kg in 2014. Consumption increased to 40 kg in 2015, remaining steady at this rate for the rest of the period.

Exercise 2

Now, read the following sentences from the graph above. There are four different parts: **'bold'**, 'CAPITALS', *'italics'* and '<u>underlined</u>' Each part has a specific function.

Read the sentences and say what you think the purpose of each different part is:

1. **To begin**, in 2001, the average number of kg of rice consumed per household per year was <u>70</u>

2. but OVER THE NEXT four years, *there was a dramatic drop to* <u>35 kg per year (annum).</u>

3. The number then *increased (grew, rose, climbed) significantly* BETWEEN 2005 AND 2006 to <u>60 kg per year (per annum).</u>

4. 2006 to 2009 *saw an erratic period (a fluctuation) in the amount of rice consumed*

5. **which was followed by** *a sharp rise* at the END OF THIS PERIOD,

6. *With the figures hitting a peak (an all-time high) of* <u>75 kg</u> in 2010.

7. *It levelled off* for the NEXT YEAR,

8. **but then**, *the average consumption plummeted, hitting a low (an all-time low) of* <u>30 kg</u> in 2014.

9. Consumption *slowly increased to* <u>40 kg,</u>

10. *remaining steady* at this rate for the REST OF THE PERIOD.

You can check your answers on the next page.

Answers:

Bold	Introduces a sentence and provides tone, coherence and contrast to the text. (Connector)
CAPITALS	Gives a time reference of when something took place (Time)
Italics	Communicates any changes or non-changes to the figures
Underlined	Specifies a value or number for the change or non-change described.

Examples:

The words in **bold** are connectors, or linking words, the words in CAPITALS are the time period, the words in *italics* are the change taking place, and the <u>underlined</u> words are the value the graph is measured in (usually a number).

Connector	Time	Change or lack of change.	Value
Initially/ Firstly/ To begin,	in 2001,	the average number of kg of rice consumed per household per year was	70

Connector	Time	Change	Value
but	over the next four years	there was a dramatic drop to	35 kg per annum.

Change	Time	Value	(no connector)
The number then increased (grew, rose, climbed) significantly	between 2005 and 2006	to 60 kg per year	

This is what you should do when you need to describe changes which occur over time.

If you don't feel very confident writing about graphs yet, focus on internalizing the sentence structures from the example description at the beginning of this chapter. You can then play with them and experiment by describing different graphs until you are able to use them fluently.

Remember to stick to tried and tested structures when you describe changes. It's often very tempting to 'go with the flow' and create structures as you go along. However, if you do not begin with a solid base, it's very easy to overcomplicate sentences and paragraphs.

Wherever possible, keep it simple when dealing with data!

Structures for describing change

If you want to achieve great results, you need to learn more than just one structure for describing change. It's very important that you add an element of variety to your writing when you are describing shifts in data. This will not only keep your reader engaged, but it will also help to demonstrate a higher level of knowledge and will give a better impression of your abilities as a communicator.

Be mindful of using the correct word forms when you are building your sentences. Lapses in concentration can cause some writers to confuse adjectives such as *progressive* with their adverb form *progressively*.

The following resource tables contain the language to describe pretty much any graph which involves changes over time.

There + be + adjective + noun + in + noun
There was a slow rise in the number of kilograms consumed.
There was a dramatic rise in the amount of oil produced.
There was a sharp jump in ice-cream sales
There has been a considerable increase in the number of languages spoken within the region since 1980.
There was a slight increase in the number of cars sold.
There was a sharp fall in the number of loans offered.
There was a dramatic fluctuation in the amount of rice consumed.

Noun + verb + adverb
Fast food consumption rose steadily.
The number of people claiming unemployment benefits rose considerably between 2008 and 2011.
The value of gold decreased slightly during the period.
The figures declined slightly, dropping to 44,000 in 2012.

Time + saw/experienced/witnessed + adjective + noun + in + noun

 *there is no preposition before time words in this structure (Never: *In* + time + *saw...*)

2003 saw a gradual increase in oil consumption.

2009 saw a sudden plunge in ice-cream sales to 20,000.

The end of the period saw a gradual decline in the figures, dropping to 44,000 in 2012.

The decade ended pretty much the same as it began, with an average consumption of just over 20lb per household.

Top Verb-Adverb Combination Examples for Describing Changes

Verb	Adverb
fell	*minimally / gradually / rapidly / dramatically / slowly / markedly / sharply*
declined	*minimally / gradually / rapidly / dramatically / slowly / markedly / sharply*
shrank	*minimally / gradually / rapidly / dramatically / slowly / markedly / sharply*
dropped	*minimally / gradually / rapidly / dramatically / slowly / markedly / sharply*
rose	*rapidly / gradually / rapidly / dramatically / slowly*
increased	*rapidly / dramatically / slowly / gradually*
grew	*slightly / steadily / suddenly / gradually*
fluctuated	*wildly / slightly / suddenly*
jumped	*erratically / slightly / dramatically*
plunged	*suddenly / unexpectedly*
soared	*suddenly / unexpectedly*

Top Combination Examples for Describing Data that Does Not Change or that Reaches a High or Low

No change

remained constant

remained flat

remained stable

levelled out

did not change

saw no change

Reached a High or a Low

reached a peak

hit a peak

hit an all-time high

reached an all-time high

bottomed out

reached a low

hit a low

hit an all-time low (during the period)

reached an all-time low (during the period)

peaked at + number, percentage or value

hit a high of/ low of + Number- percentage or value

Sentence Transformation Exercise

Use the structures for describing change above to transform each sentence.

Here are some examples for each structure we will be using in this exercise.

The + noun + verb + adverb + in + time

The consumption of bread increased gradually in 2018.

There + BE+ adjective + noun + in + noun + in + time

There was a gradual increase in the consumption of bread (in bread consumption) in 2018.

Time + saw+ adjective + noun + in + noun

2018 saw a gradual increase in the consumption of bread.

Alcohol consumption dropped suddenly during January and February.

There was a .....

January and February saw a.....

There was a slight drop in car sales during the summer period.

Car sales.....................................

The summer period saw.....................................

In May, the number of tourists increased significantly

May.....................................

There.....................................

According to the forecast, there will be a sharp increase in employment in March 2021.

March 2021 ....

Employment ....

Visits to European cities increased steadily from 2010 to 2017.

There was a ....

The period.....................................

Answers

Sentence Transformation Exercise

Alcohol consumption dropped suddenly during January and February.

There was a sudden drop in alcohol consumption during January and February.

January and February saw a sudden drop in alcohol consumption

There was a slight drop in car sales during the summer period.

Car sales dropped slightly during the summer period.

The summer period saw a slight drop in car sales

In May, the number of tourists increased significantly.

May saw a significant increase in the number of tourists.

There was a significant increase in the number of tourists in May.

There will be a sharp increase in employment in March 2021, according to the forecast (projections)..

March 2021 will see a sharp increase in employment, according to the forecast (projections).

According to the forecast (projections), employment will increase sharply in March 2021.

Visits to European cities increased steadily from 2010 to 2017.

There was a steady increase in visits to European cities from 2010 to 2017.

The period from 2010 to 2017 saw a steady increase in visits to European cities.

Exercise

Here is a similar graph. The topic is slightly different, and so is the data. **Write some sentences describing the different patterns on the graph, making sure you vary your sentence structures between the three examples we´ve looked at.**

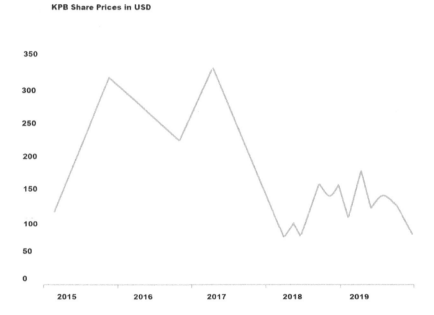

KPB Share Prices in USD

Describe the graph here

....

....

....

....

....

....

....

....

....

....

....

....

....

....

Model answer

The graph shows the changes and the overall decline in the share price of KPB over a five-year period from 2015 to 2019.

At the beginning of the period the share price was at USD 130 per share. Between 2015 and 2016 there was a sudden increase from USD 210 to USD 310 per share towards the beginning of the second year. The share price quickly dropped again throughout 2016, but it recovered, rising strongly again at the beginning of 2017 and hitting an all-time high of 320 USD per share. However, from mid-2017 there was a sharp downward trend until the beginning of the next year when it fell to the lowest point in this period at just over USD 70 per share. After that the share price recovered and, despite some fluctuations, continued to rise until it reached a price of USD 170 in early 2019. Until late 2019 the trend was downward again, ending the year at just over USD 75.

KPB made significant gains and losses during this period but overall lost around USD 100 per share.

Describing Graph Data

Look at the following graph and analyze both the descriptions.

You should spend about 20 minutes on this task.

The line graph below shows changes in fast food consumed in the UK between 1990 and 2010.

Summarize the information by selecting and reporting the main features and make comparisons where relevant.

Write at least 150 words.

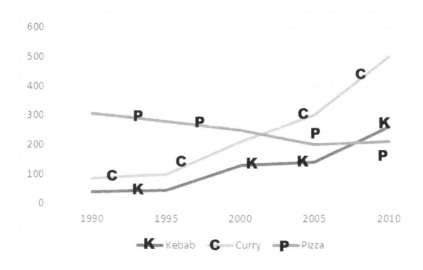

Option 1:

The graph illustrates shifts in the weekly amounts of fast food consumed in the UK between 1990 and 2010. Several trends are apparent. Firstly, the UK population are eating more and more fast food. Secondly, the type of fast food has changed.

In 1990, the most popular fast food was pizza. Over 300g were consumed each week. By 2010, however, this had fallen to just over 200g - a 50% drop. Consumption of other fast foods such as curries and kebabs increased, however. The number of kebabs eaten shot up from about 20g a week to more than 270g, overtaking pizza in the late 2000s. Curry consumption also increased, rising from about 90g in 1990 to 500g in 2010.

Accompanying this change in the choice of foods was an overall increase in the amount of fast food consumed. In 1990, British consumers ate about 330g a week of fast food. In 2010, on the other hand, this had more than tripled, to almost 950g.

Option 2:

The graph shows the amount of fast food eaten between 1990 and 2010 in grams per person per week. Overall, the amount of fast food consumed more than tripled during the period.

The amount of pizza eaten declined drastically. In 1990, the consumption was about 300g/week. This fell to 220g/week by 2010.

In contrast, sales of kebabs and curries rocketed. In 1990, relatively few kebabs were consumed - less than 20g/week. This rose to 270g/week by 2010. In the same period, curry sales shot up by more than 500%, from 90g/week in 1990 to 500 grams in 2010.

In conclusion, although there was a big increase in the consumption of curry and kebabs, sales of pizza decreased.

Analysis:

In the introduction, you should state clearly what the graph is about.

Step 1: State clearly what the graph is about

This part of the introduction must answer the following questions:

1. What type of graph are we describing?

2. What is the information?

3. How is this information measured? (i.e. millions of pounds, kg, meters, liters etc..)

4. Is there a time period? If so, what is it?

Your secret weapon here is to use paraphrasing. Paraphrase the title of the graph and the labels from the x and y axis.

Title: Changes in average weekly fast food consumption in the UK between 1990 and 2010.

Introduction 1: <u>The graph illustrates shifts in the weekly amounts of fast food consumed in the UK between 1990 and 2010.</u> Several trends are apparent. Firstly, the UK population are eating more and more fast food. Secondly, the type of fast food has changed.

Title: Changes in average weekly fast food consumption in the UK between 1990 and 2010.

Introduction 2: <u>The graph shows the amount of fast food eaten between 1990 and 2010 in grams per person per week.</u> Overall, the amount of fast food consumed more than tripled during the period.

Notes

Use the **present simple** to introduce what the graph is about. Remember you will switch to **past simple** to describe the graph.

Never use the same verb as the question. Use verbs like these to introduce the graph:

- *The graph illustrates...*
- *The graph shows ...*
- *The graph depicts...*
- *The graph compares ...*
- *The graph represents ...*

Exercise 1

Now analyze the following three graphs. Write one (or more) sentences, paraphrasing the title to explain what the graph is about.

a) *The graph shows the average number of fashion accessories purchased per year by men and women in the USA from 2016 to 2019.*

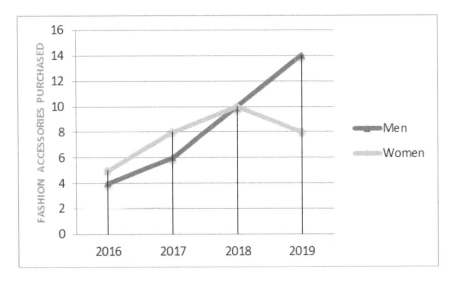

....
....
....
....
....
....

b) The line graph gives information about the number of visitors to three Australian beaches between June and September 2019.

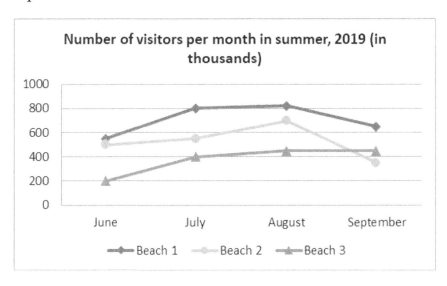

Number of visitors per month in summer, 2019 (in thousands)

....
....
....
....
....
....

c) The graph shows the population change between 1970 and 2010 in three different towns.

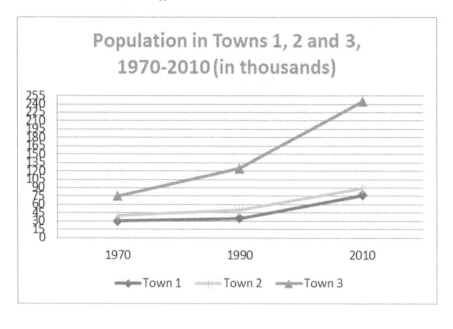

....
....
....
....
....
....

Possible Answers:

a) The graph provides data about how many fashion accessories males and females purchased every year on average in the US between 2016 and 2019.

b) The graph illustrates how many people visited three different Australian beaches during the summer of 2019.

c) The graph depicts the rise in population of Town 1, Town 2 and Town 3, from 1970 to 2010.

Step 2: Give an Overview of the Period

What are the most important things that have happened? After you have introduced the graph, you need to identify one or sometimes two main patterns or trends.

It´s particularly important to have an overview, so that the readers or listeners can read or hear the most important information straight away. It gives them a general idea of what situation is, has been or will be.

Overview	**Example 1:** *"Overall, the amount of fast food consumed more than tripled during the period."* **Example 2:** *"Several trends are apparent. Firstly, the UK population are eating more and more fast food. Secondly, the type of fast food that they eat has changed."*

Notice that the overview examples above don´t mention any statistical information about the graph (i.e. numbers, percentages, figures etc..). If you mention specific data, it may cause confusion in some cases, as some people may jump to conclusions before you finish describing.

Recommendation: Always include the 'overview' in the introduction because if you run out of time in the presentation or if someone doesn´t read your full report or email, then you will not have communicated the most important information at all.

Exercise 2:

Choosing Trends to Discuss

In order to write a good overview, you need to first, choose the key features.

This exercise will test your ability to identify the most important features in a data source correctly. Look at the following graphs and decide what the key features are for each.

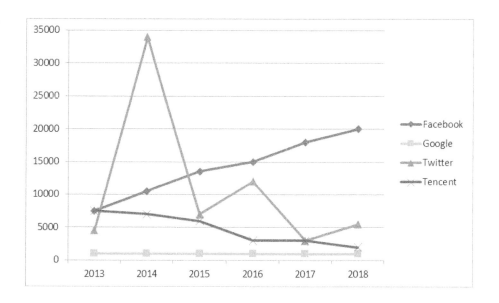

The graph above shows the stock price of four companies between 2013 and 2018. **Choose 2-4 key features to include in your overview.**

1. ....

2. ....

3. ....

4. ....

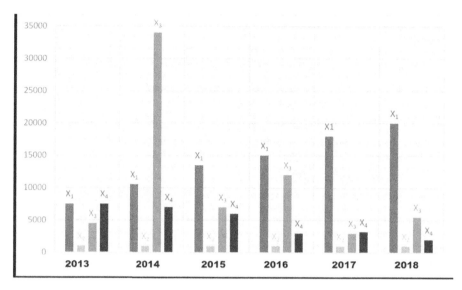

X1 Facebook X2 Google X3 Twitter X4 Tencent

The graph above shows the stock price of four companies between 2013 and 2018. **Choose 2-4 key features to include in your overview.**

1. ....

2. ....

3. ....

4. ....

Answers:

1. Graph:

Basically, the key features of this graph are that Facebook increased, Tencent decreased, Twitter fluctuated, and Google remained relatively stable.

Many students overcomplicate this type of graph. In the majority of cases, with line graphs and bar charts, the easiest or most obvious answer is the right answer.

The main objective of this kind of graph is to demonstrate the general trends over time and this is exactly what the examiners are looking for in the overview.

2- Bar Chart:

You knew it was a trick question! The information is exactly the same as in line graph 1, and therefore the key features are the same. Remember that all you are looking at is data. It doesn't matter how the data is visually represented, focus on the data itself.

Language

Historical data in a graph with dates: Although the present simple is probably the easiest – safest option to use, try to use the active, past simple to describe completed past events

If a graph has no date: you can use past or present, but your use of tenses must be consistent, so if you decide to use the present simple to describe data in a graph, you must use the present simple throughout the whole graph.

Future events and forecasts: If you are describing forecasts you need to use future tenses.

You can use phrases such as these to introduce the main points. Never try to memorize all of the phrases – choose one you like- learn it and use it every time.

Generally speaking........ x was the most striking feature.

It is very clear from the overall trend that

It can be seen from the graph that ....

The most striking feature was the ...

It is important to note that ...

It can be observed from the graph that...

Exercise 3

Look at the following graph from exercise 1 again. Write one or two sentences that identify the main key features.

Use some of these phrases for inspiration

> *Generally speaking…….. x was the most striking feature.*
>
> *It is very clear from the overall trend that*
>
> *It can be seen from the graph that ….*
>
> *The most striking feature was the …*
>
> *It is important to note that …*
>
> *It can be observed from the graph that…*

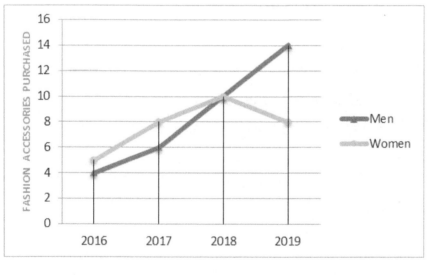

....
....
....
....
....
....

Possible Answers:

Option 1: *"The most striking feature was the* strong upward trend in the number of fashion accessories acquired by men. Although women bought more accessories than men in 2016, their average number of purchases dropped/fell/decreased/shrank to below the level of men in 2018."

Option 2: *"It can be observed from the graph that* men tended to buy more and more fashion accessories over the 4-year period, whereas the number of accessories acquired by their female counter-parts dropped/fell/decreased/shrank"

Chapter 2: Bar Charts

Organization is the Key!

Look for patterns in the data and split it into categories.

If the reader cannot understand the connection between your ideas, it will obviously have a negative impact on the quality of your writing.

To avoid communication breakdowns and to keep your text organized, divide the information into groups or categories.

For example, you could divide a list into two groups or even three groups. There is commonly one group with high numbers or values, one with mid-range numbers or values, and one with low numbers or values.

How can we group the information in this chart?

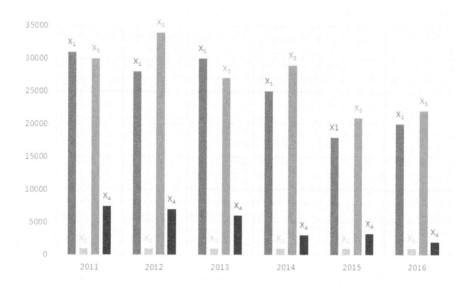

X_1 - Barley X_2 - Wheat X_3 - Hay X_4 - Rice

Group 1: ....

Group 2: ....

Answer:

Possible groups are:

> ***Group 1:*** *Barley (X1) and hay (X3) (High levels of output)*

> ***Group 2:*** *Wheat (X2) and rice (X4) (Low levels of output)*

A more difficult example:

The following bar chart shows the results of research carried out by a human resources department at a large organization. The questionnaire shows the main factors affecting employee work performance among two groups: those aged 18-44 and those aged 45-60.

How can we group the information?

Remember: Look for things that can be grouped together in your description.

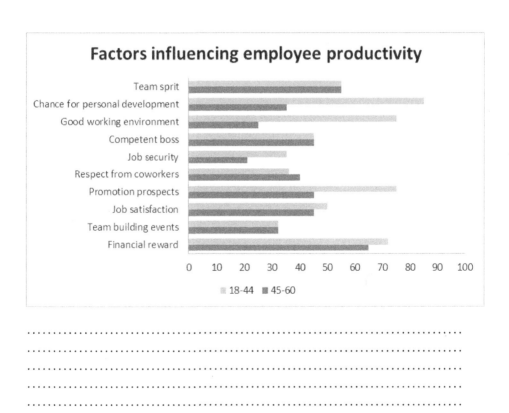

....
....
....
....
....
....
....

Answer:

This is a very difficult example since most of the time you will be able to group the information by results. For example: around group 1 40,000, group 2 around 60,000 etc…

In this case we will need to group them by type of factor. Internal or external.

For example: *"The research results show that both internal and external factors play a key role in motivating employees within the company. The internal factors that stand out are having a competent boss, team spirit, job satisfaction and respect from coworkers. The main external factors are opportunities for personal development, job security, the prospect of promotion and financial reward".*

Language

As mentioned earlier, to write a high-level description, you need to group the information together in some way. This will help build the different paragraphs for your text.

You should demonstrate your understanding of how parts are connected to each other. Therefore, you will not be using any language of change in most bar charts, instead you will be comparing and contrasting the information.

	Example	Comparative	Superlative
1 Syllable	High/Low/ Cold/Wet	Higher/Lower/Colder/Wetter	The highest/lowest/ coldest/wettest
3 or more syllables	Effective/ Popular	More Effective/ Popular	The most effective/ popular
Ending in -y	Healthy/Early	Healthier/Earlier	The healthiest/ earliest
Irregular adjectives	Bad/ Little (for quantity)	Worse/ Less	The worst/ least

Grammar Tools:

1. Comparatives are made with *more* or *-er*, but not both.

The weather is getting **warmer**. *(NOT ~~… more warmer.~~)*

Please try to be **more polite**. *(NOT ~~… more politer.~~)*

2. Use superlatives to compare people and things with the groups that they belong to.

Jessica is the tallest of the five girls. (NOT ~~Jessica is the taller of the five girls.~~)

I think I'm the oldest person in the class.

Adding Transitions into Your Sentences

Russia exports over 1.2 billion tons of timber every year. **In contrast**, the Republic of Ireland exports only around 120 thousand per year.

Iraq produced large amounts of oil. **In comparison**, Taiwan produced very little.

Germany imports some 80 million tons of rice per year; **but** produces none.

Note: remember the word *some* can be used to mean *about/ around*, so you can use it to add some variety into your writing.

While/Whereas/Although/Though

These words are great for adding transitions within sentences without having to add a full stop and write a new sentence. They allow you to compare and contrast, while keeping your text fluid and readable.

Although Italy produces over 6 million tons of olives, Spain produces almost double that amount.

Spain produces high levels of solar power, **whereas / while** Japan produces almost none.

While Germany consumes nearly 80 million tons of rice per year, it produces none.

Comparing and Contrasting Similar Data

Austria produced **the same** amount of butter as Switzerland.

Like Thailand, Malaysia produces 30,000 bottles.

India consumes over 100 million tons of rice per year; **Likewise/ Similarly**, China consumes 118.8 million.

Both India and China consume over 100 million tons of rice per year.

Both the UK and Spain produce medium levels of carbon emissions.

Chart Analysis

The following chart provides information regarding the fertility in births per woman in the six largest European economies between 2010 and 2020.

Write a report for a university lecturer describing the information in the chart.

- You should write at least 150 words.

- You should spend about 20 minutes on this task

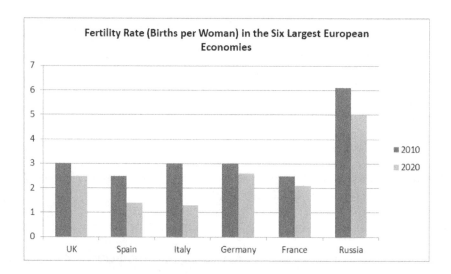

Exercise 1:

To help you analyze the graph, answer the following questions:

1. *What is the graph showing?*

2. *What measurements are used?*

3. *Is there a timeframe?*

4. *What is/are the main trend/s?*

5. *How could you group the information (look for any similarities between the patterns in the countries)?*

6. *Based on your answer to number 5, how many paragraphs would you have in total?*

Check your answers on the next page…..

Answers:

1. **What is the graph showing?** The chart shows various shifts (changes) in the fertility rates of women in six European countries, namely the UK, Spain, Italy, France, Germany and Russia between 2010 and 2020.

2. **What measurements are used?** Births per woman

3. **Is there a timeframe?** Yes (Years)

4. **What is/are the main trend/s?** there were significant decreases in birth rates in all countries except for Germany, but some countries in the region have double the fertility rate of others.

5. **How could you group the information (look for any similarities between the patterns in the countries)?** Fertility rates vary widely between these six European nations. Russia had the highest rates, with 6.1 births per woman in 2010. This compared with around 3 births per woman in the UK, Italy and Germany and just 2.5 in Spain and France.

6. **Based on your answer to number 5, how many paragraphs would you have in total?** 3-4 including the introduction

Sample Answer

Now we will look at a sample answer for the fertility rates chart.

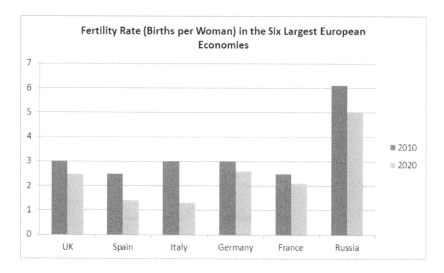

Sample Answer:

The chart represents changes in the fertility rates of female members of the population (women) in the top six European economies, namely the UK, Spain, France, Germany, Italy and Russia between 2010 and 2020. Overall it can be seen that, there were falls in birth rates in all (six) nations, although some countries in the region have (retain) much higher fertility rates than others.

There was a wide variation in birth rates between the six nations in 2010. Russia had the highest rates, with over six births per woman. This compared with around 3 births per woman in the UK, Germany and Italy, and 2.5 in France and Spain.

By the year 2020, the figures (numbers or rates) had dropped by over 50% in Italy, which registered similar rates to Spain and France at well under (below) 2.5 births per woman. Similarly, the rates shrank by over 16%, from 6.1 to 5 in Russia, while the UK and Germany also reported less births per woman with 2.5 and 2.7 respectively.

Chapter 3: Describing Two Graphs Simultaneously

When there are 2 graphs it can seem harder than just one, but it isn't.

- Look at the first, summarize it then move to the second and compare it

- Write about both equally

- Make an effective plan by either addressing each paragraph then comparing them or choosing criteria and then comparing both charts in each paragraph.

Strategy

An effective strategy is to look at the graphs then ask yourself these questions:

1. What do they have in common?

2. What is different between them?

3. What are the most interesting results and the clearest trends in each graph?

4. What conclusions can you draw from both charts?

Understanding 2 graphs: Practice

Answer questions 1-3 about the following graphs.

The chart below shows the percentage of US teens and adults consuming an average of at least 200g of fast food per day in 2017.

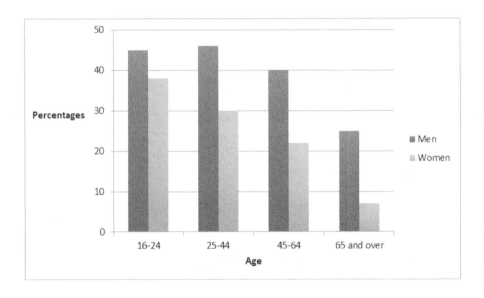

The graph below shows the average daily consumption of fast food among children, aged 10-15, in the US. (2010-2017) measured in grams.

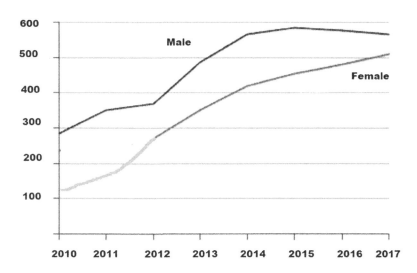

1. Which of the following statements do the 2 graphs NOT have in common:

    i.   Both show fast food consumption in the US.

    ii.   Both show the difference between the two sexes.

    iii.   Both show the similarities between the two sexes.

    iv.   Both show that males eat more fast food than females.

2. What are the clearest trends in graph 1?

3. What are the clearest trends in graph 2?

Answers:

1. Both graphs show the similarities between the two sexes.

2. In each age group men drank more than women.

   Nearly half of all males aged 16-44 exceeded 200g per day

   The highest percentage of females who eat at least 200g of fast food per day are aged between 16 and 24.

   Almost half as many women aged 45-64 (22%) exceeded 200g per day compared to the 18-24 age group (38%).

3. Between 2010 and 2017 there was a significant increase in both sexes.

   Boys ate more fast food than girls, but BOTH have increased since 2010.

   Between 2012 and 2014 there was a significant increase in both sexes.

   The number of grams eaten by girls increased almost five-fold between 2010 and 2017.

   The number of grams started to decrease for boys after 2015.

   The gap between boys and girls became narrower.

Sample Answer 2

Graph Description:

Write a report describing the information below.

Write at least 150 words.

The first chart shows the percentage of US teens and adults consuming an average of at least 200g of fast food per day in 2017.

The second graph shows the average daily consumption of fast food among children, aged 10-15, in the US. (2010-2017) measured in grams.

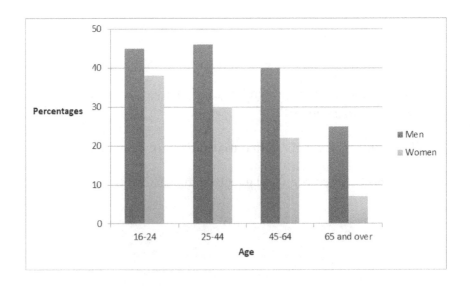

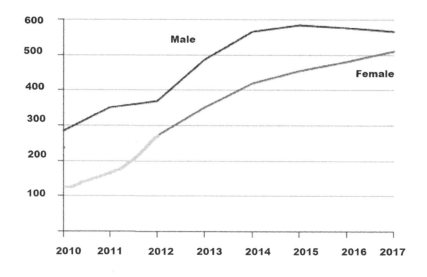

Model Answer:

Both charts show the levels of fast food consumption in children and adults in the USA.

The bar chart displays the difference in percentages between teen and adult males and females in 2017, **while the second graph shows** the daily number of grams consumed by girls and boys aged 10-15 between 2010 and 2017.

The first chart shows that nearly 50% of all males aged 16-44 consumed more than 200g of fast food on a daily basis. Although the numbers were also relatively high for females aged 16-24 (38%), the figures for those aged 25-64 were approximately half **that of** their male counterparts. **In addition**, the percentage of women over 65 was dramatically lower at just 7% as opposed to (compared to) around 25% of men.

The second chart reveals that there was a substantial rise in fast food consumption among children (both boys and girls) **between** 2010 **and** 2017. In fact, the number of grams they ate approximately doubled for males increased five-fold for females. The sharpest rises occured from 2012 to 2015, **increasing to** 580g and 460g for boys and girls respectively. **Since** 2015 the figure has dropped slightly for boys but for girls it has continued to grow, **hitting a peak** of **just above** 500g in 2017.

Language Note:

Synonyms for *similar to* are

Akin to

Analogous to

You can use the combination *that of* to compare situations and figures. For example, in the model answer we wrote *"the figures for those aged 25-64 were approximately half* **that of** *their male counterparts"*, to mean *"the figures for those aged 25-64 were approximately half* **the figures of** *their male counterparts"* . The second option is also fine, but it can sound a bit repetitive if you do it too much. This is why we are using *that of* here.

That of can also be used to compare situations or contexts. Let's look at the following two sentences. Is there a difference in meaning? If so, what is that difference?

Sentence 1: The situation is akin **to** a bus in rush hour traffic.

Sentence 2: The situation is akin **to that of** a bus in rush hour traffic.

In the first sentence, you are comparing a situation to a bus journey in rush hour traffic, or to the bus itself, it's not entirely clear. *That of* is used in the second sentence to specify that you are referring to the situation the bus is in, not the bus itself or anything else that could be interpreted from the first sentence.

Chapter 4: Pie Charts

Write a report describing the information below.

- You should write at least 150 words.
- You should spend about 20 minutes on this task.

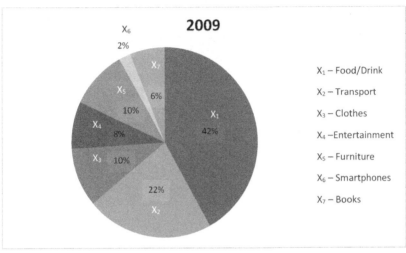

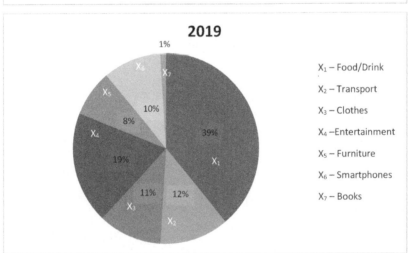

How to organize your answer

In which order should you present the information?

Here you have two options:

1. Describe the chart in 2009 and then describe the information presented for 2019.

2. Write about both pie charts simultaneously, comparing each activity in turn.

Which way you choose to answer the question depends on how comfortable you feel with the description. The first method is probably the safest and easiest option of the two, but it can also be slightly boring and doesn´t allow you to display such a wide range of language and structures.

In addition, Method 1 doesn´t allow the reader to make immediate direct comparisons between the same categories. For example, with Method 1, if the reader wants to know how the use of transport has changed between 2009 and 2019, they have to read the whole description.

Students who are able to use Method 2 appropriately usually get the highest grades in the exam.

The first thing you should mention in your pie chart description

When you are describing the pie chart, the most relevant information is usually in the biggest 'portions' of the chart or the parts which have changed the most during the time period.

In the example, you should start by writing about food/drink, transport, entertainment, smartphones and books.

You should start by writing about food/drink, transport, entertainment, smartphones and books, because they show significant variations, whereas furniture and clothes should hold less focus because they show only small changes.

What should you include in the overview

This is the same as in the line graph and bar chart, you should always focus your overview on the most important changes or differences.

What language should you use?

If the pie chart describes changes which happen over time you should use language to describe changes and compare and contrast. Nevertheless, not all pie charts describe changes which happened over time, so check before you start writing.

Percentages and Proportions

While not all pie charts describe changes which happened over time, all pie charts display percentages and proportions, so you need to review the language for fractions and percentage. You can find a resource bank for this language after the next exercise.

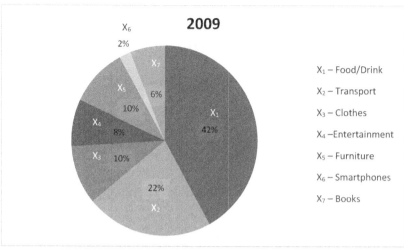

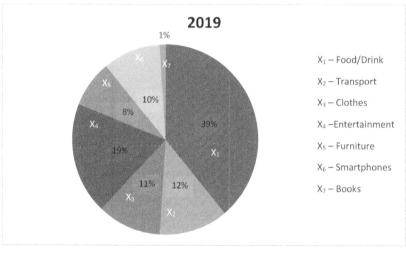

Sample Answer:

Put the words in brackets into the correct form.

The pie charts 1........... (display) changes in UK spending patterns from 2009 to 2019.

Food/drink and transport 2.......... (make up) the two main items of expenditure in 2009, both 3................

(comprise) over 60% of household spending. Food and drink 4......... (account) for 42% of spending that year, but this 5......... (shrink) to 39% in 2019. Furthermore, while spending on transport plummeted from 22% in 2009 to 12% in 2019, spending on entertainment more than 6........ (double), 7.......... (increase) from 8% in 2009 to 19% in 2019.

Interestingly, as spending on books 8......... (fall) 9............ (drastic), 10...........(slide) from 6% to 1%, the percentage of outlay spent on smartphones 11.............. (skyrocket), up from 2% in 2009 to 10% in 2019.

Some areas 12.......... (remain) 13............. (relative) 14............. (change). Britons 15.......... (spend) 16.......... (approximate) the same amount of salary on clothes and furniture in both years.

In conclusion, there were 17........... (relative) high 18.......... (increase) in the amounts spent on entertainment and smartphones at the expense of food, transport and books.

Answers:

1. display

2. made up

3. comprising

4. accounted for

5. shrank

6. doubled,

7. increasing

8. fell

9. drastically

10. sliding

11. skyrocketed

12. remained

13. relatively

14. unchanged.

15. spent

16. approximately

17. relatively

18. increases

You must demonstrate a variety of language.

Using a variety of fractions and percentages can add perspective to your data description. Presenting something as *two thirds*, or as *over half* of the total, can really increase your reader's interest, as it provides context and perspective to the data you are presenting. It also adds variety, which stops your writing from becoming predictable and monotonous.

In addition, you can use phrases to show when a number is not exact, such as 'some', 'around', 'roughly', 'just under', 'slightly over', or 'just over' for example.

Percentages & Fractions

5% /   one in twenty

10% /   one in ten

15% /   under one fifth (to express that this figure is small)

15% /   almost one fifth (to express that this figure is large)

20% /   one fifth

25% /   one quarter

30% /   under one third (to express that this figure is small)

30% /   nearly one third (to express that this figure is large)

35% /   over one third

40% /   two-fifths

45% /   over two fifths

50% /   half

55% /   over half

60% /   three-fifths

65% /   two-thirds

70% /   seven in ten

75% /   three-quarters

80% /   four-fifths

Mini Exercise

Choose a qualifier from the list below and use it with a fraction to express the percentage on the left. The first one has been done for you as an example.

just over/ almost / approximately/ ~~nearly~~/ over

Percentage = Qualifier + Fraction

59% =   *nearly three-fifths*

52% =

26% =

78% =

39% =

Answers

Percentage = Qualifier + Fraction

59% =   nearly three-fifths

52% =   just over half

26% =   approximately a quarter

78% =   over two-thirds

39% =   almost four-fifths

Exercise:

Pie Charts which Compare Past and Future

Use the lists of words 1-4 below to write your own sentences to describe a pie chart. Add the relevant data in brackets and change the verb tenses accordingly.

1. Electric cars/account for (20%)/ traffic volume/ in 2015/ while/ in 2050/ forecast/represent (45%).

2. Estimate/success/rate/2025/(35%)/in contrast/to (63%)/2015.

3. in/ 2006/ laptops/ make up/ bulk/ devices/ (94%) used/ but/ 2021/ this forecast/ drop to (20%)

1. ....
   ....

2. ....
   ....

3. ....
   ....

Answers:

1. Electric cars accounted for 20% of traffic volume in 2015 while in 2050 it is forecast to represent 55%.

2. It is estimated that success rate will fall to 35% in 2025 in contrast to 63% in 2015.

3. In 2006 laptops made up the bulk of devices used (94%), but by 2021, this is forecast to drop to 20%.

Chapter 5: Tables

You don´t need to learn any new language to successfully describe a table. When you start the task, you need to look for data that you can group together, as you would do in any other description.

Always start with the most interesting information (often the biggest things) and leave the least interesting data until the end of the description.

Exercise 1

Re-write sentences a-i using the language in the box below. You can make any necessary changes. There are four extra expressions you won´t need to use.

The bulk of

the lowest percentages

was noticeably higher

a smaller proportion of

was significantly higher

had the lowest percentages

had slightly higher figures

a third of the number of

40% of

Over 75%

Three times the number of

the largest proportion of

One in four

a. The Iron Maiden concert was attended by three times as many people as the Stone Temple Pilots concert.

b. More than four out of ten people chose to use public transport.

c. The largest proportion of purchases came from China as opposed to the E.U.

d. A quarter of customers ordered digital rather than traditional print products.

e. The social media platform lost just under three quarters of its visitors when compared to last year.

f. Consumers in all countries spent more on food, drinks and tobacco than on any other product category.

g. Consumers spent the least on leisure/education in all countries.

h. Consumers in Turkey and Ireland spent quite a lot more on food, drinks and tobacco than consumers in the other countries.

i. Spending on clothing and footwear was a lot higher in Italy, at 9%, than in the rest of the countries.

a. ....
....

b. ....
....

c. ....
....

d. ....
....

e. ....
....

f. ....
....

g. ....
....

h. ....
....

i. ....
....

Suggested Answers

a. The Iron Maiden concert was attended by **three times the number of** many people as the Stone Temple Pilots concert.

b. More than **40% of** people chose to use public transport.

c. **The bulk of** purchases came from China as opposed to the E.U.

d. **One in four** customers ordered digital rather than traditional print products.

e. The social media website lost just **under 75%** of its visitors when compared to last year.

f. **The largest proportion** of spending in all countries was on food, drinks and tobacco.

g. The leisure/education category has **the lowest percentages** in the table.

h. Consumer spending on food, drinks and tobacco **was noticeably higher** in Turkey and Ireland than in the other countries.

i. Spending on clothing and footwear **was significantly higher** in Italy, at 9%, than in the rest of the countries.

Tables can look intimidating if you don´t know where to start, but a table with a time measurement is no different to a line graph. If the table has no time measurement, then we would use exactly the same description as with a bar chart (one that is not measured in time).

Sample Table

Consumer spending for three categories in 5 US Cities in 2019

City	Food	Alcohol	Leisure
New York	26.21%	7.43%	3.11%
Los Angeles	16.36%	8.51%	3.38%
Chicago	18.8%	7.51%	1.89%
Atlanta	13.91%	7.01%	2.98%
Miami	34.59%	7.22%	8.28%

Fill the blanks with the correct word, words or phrase.

The table .... for three categories of products and services in New York, Los Angeles, Chicago, Atlanta and Miami in 2019.

Overall, it can be seen that..................................... was on food. On the other hand, the leisure category has the ....

Consumer spending on food was ...., at 26.21%, and almost 35% .... The percentage of consumer spending on leisure products and services was also greatest in Miami, at 8.28%, while spending on alcohol ...., at 8.51%, than in the rest of the cities.

Atlanta had .... for food, at
.... 14%, and for alcohol, at .... 7%.
Chicago, on the other hand, had slightly more elevated levels of spending for these categories, but the lowest percentage for leisure, at
.... 2%.

Suggested Answer

The table reveals proportions of consumer spending for three categories of products and services in New York, Los Angeles, Chicago, Atlanta and Miami in 2019.

Overall, it can be seen that the largest percentage of spending in all cities was on food. On the other hand, the leisure category has the lowest percentages in the table.

Consumer spending on food was noticeably higher in New York and Miami, at 26.21%, and almost 35% respectively. The percentage of consumer spending on leisure products and services was also greatest in Miami, at 8.28%, while spending on alcohol was higher in Los Angeles, at 8.51%, than in the rest of the cities.

Atlanta had the lowest spending levels for food, at just under/below 14%, and for alcohol, at just above/over 7%. Chicago, on the other hand, had slightly more elevated levels of spending for these categories, but the lowest percentage for leisure, at slightly under/below 2%.

Chapter 6: Process Description

Describing Sequences

In business, you will sometimes have to describe the process of something to a client, to colleague or to a manager. Describing a process, may require you to have basic knowledge of the language and workings of certain scientific, engineering or other technical matters. While these can be easily learnt in many cases, the glue that holds the process description together is the type of language and structure you use when you communicate your ideas.

Describing Sequences

The following linking words and phrases in the box **can** be used to describe a sequence.

before / prior to	At first / firstly/ initially
following that/ after that / next / then/ when	as soon as/ once / immediately after/ in turn
before	after
where	At the same time- simultaneously
finally	

Exercise 1:

Highlight or underline the linking words in A-G and decide which one is the first step in the sequence. Once you have done this, decide what is being described and put the sentences in order.

A. If it's being refurbished, the faulty components of the device are repaired in the factory

B. and the tablet is then returned to the shop as a refurbished product.

C. Once the device breaks, it is either discarded or refurbished.

D. They are then assembled at a different factory

E. First, the computer processors for the tablets are manufactured in an outsourced factory.

F. Then they are sent to the central warehouse for distribution around the country

G. Simultaneously, the exterior and the memory chip are produced.

Exercise 2:

Match 1 to 6 below with a sentence or phrase A-F to complete sequence descriptions. Please note that each full sentence belongs to a different description.

1. As soon as the bricks have been formed

2. After fermentation,

3. Once the oranges are ripe they are collected,

4. The water then flows into the penstock, which is a narrow chamber,

5. When the plant reaches a certain width, the leaves are picked.

6. In the early stages of milk production, cows graze in the field and subsequently (then-afterwards) taken to a milking machine twice a day.

A. the chocolate is placed into molds and left to cool down.

B. The raw product is then heated to a high temperature to kill bacteria and make it safe for human consumption. Following this, it is put into refrigeration storage.

C. and they are then spread (laid) out on a large (industrial sized) tray to enable them to dry under the sun.

D. they are left to dry.

E. they are then dried, sorted, blended and packaged ready for distribution to retailers.

F. and increases the pressure until the turbine turns.

Answers:

Exercise 1

Linking words: if, and , then, once, then, first, simultaneously.

The lifecycle of a tablet computer is being described.

E, G, D, F, C, A, B

Exercise 2

1d, 2a, 3c, 4f, 5e, 6b

Some Essential Vocabulary for Process Descriptions:

Noun	Verb
Storage	Store
Pasteurization	Pasteurize
Harvest – harvesting	Harvest
Delivery	Deliver
Assembly	Assemble
Packing -Packaging	Pack - Package

Exercise 3:

Read the process description on the next page and fill in the blanks with the missing word or phrase.

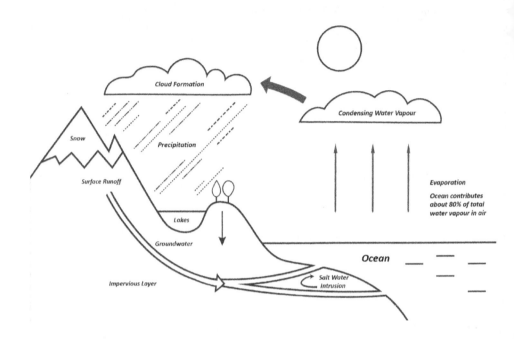

Diagram adapted from Nasa
https://gpm.nasa.gov/education/water-cycle

The diagram .... the water cycle. Firstly, water .... from the sea and floats into the atmosphere, ... **(two words)** accumulates in clouds and cools and condenses into rain or snow. The next stage shows the water's journey after falling to the ground, ... ends with .... **(three words)**

In the first stage of the ...., water, approximately 80% of which comes from Oceans, ... into the air as a result of the heat of the sun. After ...., the water vapor condenses to form clouds. An .... 80% of the water vapor comes from Oceans.

In the next ...., as clouds accumulate condensation they produce precipitation in the form of rain and snow. A large part of the water from the precipitation falls into lakes or is .... by the ground.

Part of the groundwater then .... back to the ocean without reaching the impervious layer through surface runoff.

................., Ocean water seeps through to the freshwater aquifers during the process is saltwater intrusion.

Answers:

The diagram **illustrates** the water cycle. Firstly, water **evaporates** from the sea and floats into the atmosphere, **where it** accumulates in clouds and cools and condenses into rain or snow. The next stage shows the water's journey after falling to the ground, **which** ends with **salt water intrusion.**

In the first stage of the **process**, water, approximately 80% of which comes from Oceans, **evaporates** into the air as a result of the heat of the sun. After **this**, the water vapor condenses to form clouds. An **estimated** 80% of the water vapor comes from Oceans.

In the next **stage**, as clouds accumulate condensation they produce precipitation in the form of rain and snow. A large part of the water from the precipitation falls into lakes or is **absorbed** by the ground.

Part of the groundwater then **flows** back to the ocean without reaching the impervious layer through surface runoff.

Finally, Ocean water seeps through to the freshwater aquifers during the process is saltwater intrusion.

Chapter 7: Describing Maps & Terrains

Structure

If you need to write a short description of the changes in a terrain or a map, it is usually better to use a standard structure with four paragraphs. In a presentation, this would be four sections. The four-paragraph structure helps you write a well organised description which is easier for the reader to follow.

Paragraph 1- Paraphrase Sentence

In your first paragraph you should paraphrase the basic information from the title using synonyms wherever possible.

Paragraph 2- Overview

In the overview section of your description write two general sentences about the map or terrain. You need to write about the most important differences between both maps, when you are comparing past and present situations. This would be in cases when you need to describe the changes which have taken place in an area for a report, proposal or presentation for instance.

Some examples of general sentences for a good overview are:

1. Over the time period, the area underwent radical changes

2. In the period between 1996 and 2006, the park was totally redesigned.

3. From 2008 to 2018, the city center was subject to some important developments.

4. The downtown area was completely modernized during the time period.

5. The city changed considerably over the fifteen-year period.

6. During the ten-year period, the woodland area was completely transformed.

7. Between 2007 and 2017, the old block of flats was renovated.

8. Over the time period, the church was completely refurbished.

Important questions to help you identify the main changes:

1. Were the changes big or small (major or minor)?

2. Were there any big improvements to the infrastructure of the area?

3. How did the buildings and facilities within the area change?

4. Is the area more residential than it was before or is it less residential?

5. Has the number of trees increased or decreased over time?

Paragraph 3- Main Body

You can group information together here either by location on the map or by time if you prefer. In this paragraph you should write around 4 clear and logical sentences about specific changes which occurred during the time period.

Paragraph 4- Main Body 2

In this paragraph you should write around 3 or maybe 4 clear and logical sentences about specific changes which occurred during the time period. You can group information together here either by location on the map or by time if you prefer.

Verbs to describe changes in maps

Exercise 1

Match each beginning of a sentence 1-7 with an ending A-G. More than one option may be possible.

Notice the verb phrases underlined in A-G (we will look at these later).

1. The center of the village
2. Several old houses
3. A new hospital
4. The old factories
5. Some old mills
6. Some of the trees around the old park
7. The fire station

A. <u>replaced</u> the old run-down sports center *
B. <u>were knocked down</u> <u>to make way for</u> a new park.
C. <u>were pulled down</u>, with a new hotel <u>taking their place</u>
D. <u>were demolished</u> <u>to create</u> more space which <u>was turned into</u> a campsite
E. <u>were chopped down</u> in order <u>to increase the size of</u> path.
F. <u>was converted into</u> a gym and the car park <u>torn down</u>.
G. <u>was totally transformed</u> over the fifteen-year period.

* *run-down* is an adjective which means decaying, dirty old and not taken care of.

Useful change phrases for map descriptions:

Replaced	took the place of
were knocked down to make way for	when a building or wall is deliberately destroyed to create space for something else
were pulled down	building or wall was destroyed especially because it was very old or dangerous
were demolished to create	when a building or wall is deliberately destroyed to create space for something else
was turned into	were transformed or changed into something else
were chopped down	the action of cutting trees until they fall
to increase the size of	generic term for: to make bigger or wider
to reduce the size of	generic term for: to make smaller or narrower
taking their place	occupying the place where the other thing used to be
was converted into	was transformed or changed into
was torn down	was knocked down

Exercise 2

Underline the most appropriate verb in bold in sentences 1-8 and put it into the right form to suit the sentence.

1. The abandoned car-park near the woodlands **develop/become** into a museum.

2. The area around the city center **turn into/become** less accessible with the construction of the new theatre.

3. As the city **extend/expand**, more bus stations were built.

4. A bus station **construct/ become** after the old warehouses were knocked down.

5. The downtown area of the city completely **change/demolish** with the introduction of the new shopping center.

6. A number of important developments **take place/ convert**, which totally **alter/expand** the character of the premises.

7. The area **turn into/become** more family-friendly with the **introduce/ knock down** of new parks and open spaces.

8. The road was **extend/expand** to the town center, and a new bus service was introduced to carry passengers to and from the airport.

....
....

....
....

....
....

....
....

....
....

....
....

....
....

....
....

....
....

....
....

Exercise 3:

Look at the following map task. Read the sample answer on the next page and fill in the blanks with the missing word or phrase.

Image Source: Cambridge English Practice Tests.
https://www.cambridge.org/gb/cambridgeenglish/catalog/cambridge-english-exams-ielts/resources

The two maps below show an island, before and after the construction of some tourist facilities.

Summarise the information by selecting and reporting the main features, and make comparisons where relevant.

Write at least 150 words.

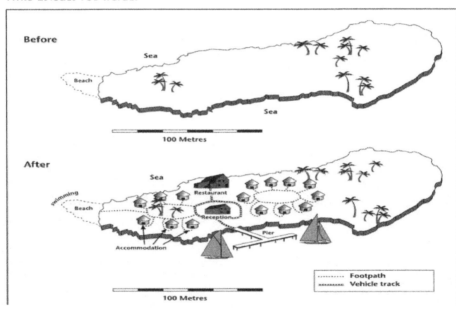

Image Source: Cambridge English Practice Tests.
https://www.cambridge.org/gb/cambridgeenglish/catalog/cambridge-english-exams-ielts/resources

Sample Answer:

The two maps illustrate the changes which have .... **(two words)** on a small island, prior to and after its development for tourism.

The introduction of tourism on the island has .... **(two words)** the landscape, with several new developments that can be seen in the second diagram. The most important changes are that the island now has ample accommodation for tourists and there is a peer to enable visitors to access the island.

One of the most striking changes are the accommodation huts which are connected by footpaths and which have been .... around the reception and restaurant area. A total of 6 huts, have been constructed in the west of the island and another 9 have been built around the center of the island.

A pier has also been developed on the south coast of the island to make the island .... to tourists and there is a short road linking it with the reception and restaurant. The trees which were scattered around the island have been left untouched, and a swimming area has been .... just off the beach.

Answers:

Exercise 1

1. G

2. B/C/D

3. A

4. B/C/D

5. B/C/D

6. E

7. A/F

Exercise 2

1. developed / was developed

2. became

3. expanded

4. was constructed

5. was completely changed / completely changed

6. took place, altered

7. became , introduction

8. was extended

Exercise 3

The two maps illustrate the changes which have taken place on a small island, prior to and after its development for tourism.

The introduction of tourism on the island has significantly changed the landscape, with several new developments that can be seen in the second diagram. The most important changes are that the island now has ample accommodation for tourists and there is a peer to enable visitors to access the island.

One of the most striking changes are the accommodation huts which are connected by footpaths and which have been built around the reception and restaurant area. A total of 6 huts, have been constructed in the west of the island and another 9 have been built around the center of the island.

A pier has also been developed on the south coast of the island to make the island accessible to tourists and there is a short road linking it with the reception and restaurant. The trees which were scattered around the island have been left untouched, and a swimming area has been designated just off the beach.

Chapter 8: How to Express Yourself in Writing

"The definition of genius is taking the complex and making it simple."

— Albert Einstein

"Simplicity is the glory of expression."

— Walt Whitman

Debunking the Myth of Complexity in Good Writing

Pause for a moment and consider your personal definition of 'good writing.'

People sometimes confuse good writing as the ability to express simple ideas in a complex manner. However, thinking this way is dangerous in business and professional contexts, as it leads to illogical and convoluted sentences that add little to the reader's understanding of a topic. To put it bluntly, it causes confusion and breaks relationships.

Therefore, when it comes to defining 'good writing,' clarity and simplicity should be at the forefront.

In reality, the biggest obstacle to improving your writing skills is the mistaken belief that 'good writing' is synonymous with complex language and intricate sentences.

Many of us have the mistaken belief that building complex sentences makes us come across as more intelligent or professional, but it has the complete opposite effect. In fact, effective writing, particularly in a professional business setting, prioritizes logic and coherence over complexity. While advanced language and complexity can be part of good writing, they must emerge naturally and appropriately from logical thinking.

'The Pyramid Method' of Writing Sentences

As we've mentioned, one of the keys to effective writing is simplicity. Overthinking your writing and building structures solely for complexity often lead to grammatical errors and lack of clarity.

Think of each sentence you write as a small house, or pyramid. Just as a pyramid needs a solid base to stand strong, your writing needs a clear foundation from which to develop. This foundation is your core message or idea, expressed in a simple, direct way. From this base, you can then build your writing, adding detail, complexity, and sophistication – much like adding rooms, floors, and decorations to a pyramid. However, if the foundation is weak, the entire structure is at risk, no matter how nicely it's decorated. The same applies to writing; without a clear, solid base, all the elaborate language and complex structures will not be able to save your piece from falling flat. Therefore, always prioritize establishing a strong foundation for your writing.

3. MOSTLY OPTIONAL:
Details, technical knowledge, or phrases to 'decorate' your writing.

2. IMPORTANT: Now, edit some sentences and words to add some variety to your writing.

1. ESSENTIAL: Start with Basic Grammar- Short, Clear Sentences. Clear Vocabulary.

The *Pyramid Method* of writing sentences.

Think of each sentence you write as a small house, or pyramid: the foundation must be solid, simple, and clear. Once you have this solid base, you can then add variety to make your text more interesting to the reader. You can add extra details or language to polish your sentences at the end, but the initial foundation must consist of a clear and direct expression of your ideas.

Remember, the basic grammar rules of English remain the same, regardless of the context. Their application should not change simply because you are writing in a professional setting.

Exercise 1:

Applying 'the Pyramid Method'

As already mentioned, writing professionally is not as hard as it may seem. Using the Pyramid Method, you can start simple, and then gradually improve your sentences.

Try the following exercise to help you improve your writing:

Instructions:

- In the following sentences, the writer has started simple (Stage 1 of The Pyramid Method).

- However, they haven't developed their sentences afterwards.

- The result is that the sentences are too personal, too informal and sound too simple for a professional document.

Task:

Use the key phrase in CAPITALS to complete the second sentence so that it means the same as the first sentence. Try to completely change the original sentence while retaining the same basic message.

1. Vegetables are good for you but meat is also good for you.

NOBODY WOULD DISPUTE THE FACT THAT...

. . . .
. . . .
. . . .

2. Newspapers lie.

IT IS PROBABLY TRUE TO SAY THAT.....

. . . .
. . . .
. . . .

3. Lots of people like chocolate because it is delicious, but it makes people fat.

FEW PEOPLE WOULD CONTEST THAT....

. . . .
. . . .
. . . .
. . . . . .

And now a particularly challenging sentence...

Tips: Remember words like *hence, therefore, as a result, in turn etc...*

4. If people have jobs they have more money so they buy more things. When people buy more things, businesses sell more things. This is good for businesses. When businesses sell more things they need more people. When businesses need more people they employ them, so more people get jobs and have money to spend. It´s a circle of capitalist awesomeness.

ALL THE EVIDENCE SUGGESTS THAT......

....

....

....

......

Suggested Answers:

1. **Nobody would dispute the fact that** vegetables have a positive impact on health, **however** meat is also vital **in order to** maintain a healthy and balanced lifestyle.

2. **It is probably true to say that** newspapers and other media often distort the truth.

3. **Few people would contest that** chocolate is very popular due to its taste, however it can often lead to obesity and other health issues.

4. **All the evidence suggests that** an increase in the level of employment would lead to higher levels of spending (which would benefit businesses) and **in turn** increase employment further as businesses would seek to meet the increase in demand.

OR

All the evidence suggests that an increase in the level of employment would lead to higher levels of spending (which would benefit businesses). This, **in turn**, would increase employment (further) as businesses would seek to meet the increase in demand.

Exercise 2

Fill the gaps with an appropriate word or phrase from the box:

To conclude	I hold the view that	however.	Firstly, research suggests that
may	which can lead to	For instance,	when people
they are more likely to	Secondly, few people would contest that	Therefore	it is likely that
Finally,	such as	However, there are those who argue that	nobody would contest the fact that
In addition, it is often claimed that	Nobody would dispute the fact that	there can be no doubt that	Hence,

Model Text

.... many programs on television include violent scenes, especially action and horror movies. .... they should not be allowed, ... many people disagree with this opinion. In this essay, I will discuss both sides and give reasons for my opinion.

.........**,** .... people who watch violent programs and play violent computer games .... worry more about their own safety, ... problems in society.

...................**,** .... are worried about their safety, ... react aggressively towards strangers. .... some children copy what they see on television and in computer games. ...... if they are watching and interacting with violence on a daily basis ....

they will copy this type of behavior. ...., there are more beneficial activities that children could be participating in, ... playing a sport or reading a book.

.... violence is not something we learn from television and computer games. For example, ... there were murders before television and videogames were invented. ....,

.... children cannot watch violent programs and play inappropriate videogames easily. For instance, there are restrictions for some programs and games, and many parents do not allow their children to watch television after a certain time.

.... , although there are some reasonable arguments against higher restrictions on violent videogames and programs for children, ... the potential disadvantages of children copying what they see and hear in these programs and games far outweigh the advantages of having free access to them. Furthermore, current restrictions are ineffective and easy to ignore. .... , governments and local institutions should do more to promote alternative activities and to engage young people in their local communities from an early age.

Answers:

Nobody would dispute the fact that many programs on television include violent scenes, especially action and horror movies. **I hold the view that** they should not be allowed, **however** many people disagree with this opinion. In this essay, I will discuss both sides and give reasons for my opinion.

Firstly, **research suggests that** people who watch violent programs and play violent computer games **may** worry more about their own safety, **which can lead to** problems in society. **For instance**, **when people** are worried about their safety, **they are more likely to** react aggressively towards strangers. **Secondly**, **few people would contest that** some children copy what they see on television and in computer games. **Hence**, if they are watching and interacting with violence on a daily basis **it is likely that** they will copy this type of behavior. **Finally**, there are more beneficial activities that children could be participating in **such as** playing a sport or reading a book.

However, there are those who argue that violence is not something we learn from television and computer games. For example, **nobody would contest the fact that** there were murders before television and videogames were invented. **In addition**, **it is often claimed that** children cannot watch violent programs and play inappropriate videogames easily. For instance, there are restrictions for some programs and games, and many parents do not allow their children to watch television after a certain time.

To conclude, although there are some reasonable arguments against higher restrictions on violent videogames and programs for children, **there can be no doubt that** the potential disadvantages of children copying what they see and hear in these programs and games far outweigh the advantages of having free access to them. Furthermore, current restrictions are ineffective and easy to ignore. **Therefore**, governments and local institutions should do more to promote alternative activities and to engage young people in their local communities from an early age.

The Connection Between Clear Thinking and Effective Writing

There's a relationship between clear thinking and effective writing. The clarity of your thoughts translates into the clarity of your writing. If your thinking is clear, your writing will naturally follow suit. On the other hand, muddled thinking often results in confusing and ineffective writing. Therefore, before you start writing, take the time to organize your thoughts, define your message, and understand what you want to convey. This process will help you write more clearly and effectively.

The 7-Step Tool: **Clarity of Thought and Writing**

Follow these steps to ensure that your clear thinking translates into effective, clear writing.

1. Identify Your Core Message: Before you even begin writing, identify the main point or message you want to convey. This will serve as your guide for all your writing efforts.

2. Brainstorm: Write all the ideas, arguments, examples, or points that you think are relevant to your core message.

Don't worry about the order or clarity at this stage; the idea is to get everything out of your head and onto paper.

3. Organize Your Thoughts: Look at the ideas you've written. Are there any themes or categories emerging?

Try to group related ideas together.

This can help you identify the key points that support your core message.

4. Create a Logical Flow: Determine the order in which you want to present your key points. Remember, a logical progression can make your writing more compelling and easier to understand.

5. Define Your Message: Now that you have your key points and their order, write a clear, concise statement of your overall message or argument.

6. Draft Your Piece: Start writing your piece, keeping your organized thoughts and defined message in mind.

Aim for clarity and simplicity in your language.

7. Review and Refine: After you've written your first draft, take the time to review it. Does your writing effectively convey your core message? Are your thoughts presented in a clear and logical way?

Make revisions as necessary to improve clarity and coherence.

Techniques for Clear and Direct Writing

Simplifying your writing doesn't mean making it too simple; it's about making your writing more accessible to your readers.

Here are some general guidelines to follow:

- **Use Simple Words**: Wherever possible, opt for simpler words over complex ones. For example, use 'use' instead of 'utilize', 'help' instead of 'facilitate'.

- **Be Concise**: Avoid unnecessary words or phrases that don't add value to your message. Every word should serve a purpose.

- **Use Active Voice:** Active voice makes your writing more direct and clear. It shows who is doing what, making it easier for readers to understand.

- **Keep Sentences Short**: Short sentences are generally easier to understand than long ones. Aim for an average of 15-20 words per sentence.

- **Use Simple Sentence Structures:** Use subject-verb-object structures as much as possible.

- **Avoid Excessive Subordination:** Too many clauses can make a sentence confusing. If a sentence has more than one or two clauses, consider breaking it up.

Even complex ideas can be expressed simply. Here's how:

Break Down Complex Ideas: Divide complex ideas into smaller, more digestible parts. Explain each part individually before connecting them back to the larger idea.

Use Analogies and Metaphors: These can help make complex ideas more relatable and easier to understand.

Use Concrete Examples: Abstract ideas can be made more understandable by providing concrete examples or case studies.

Stick to Basic Grammar

Grammar is the backbone of any language. It lends credibility to your writing and helps effectively convey your message. Whether you're writing an informal email or a detailed business report, adhering to basic grammar rules is essential. Poor grammar can cause misunderstandings and can negatively impact the perception of your professionalism and credibility.

For example, confusing "its" and "it's" or "there", "their", and "they're" can lead to misinterpretation, in some cases, and can distract the reader from your main message.

Word Order

Exercise

Where you choose to arrange words in a sentence communicates their relationship. If feasible, keep words and groups of words connected in meaning and separate the ones that don't share a close connection.

Example:

There's a large reservoir in the area that we need to build around.

Should read:

We need to build around a large reservoir in the area.

The following sentences are wrong. Rewrite them by reorganizing the words to make them clearer. You can check the suggested answers on the next page.

1. The results of the survey, which were quite surprising, were presented to us by the research team last Friday.

2. To the annual conference, where he won an award for his innovative work, the young scientist travelled all the way from Germany.

3. James, who is my colleague, and I will be leading the new project that the board approved last week.

4. With her team, Mary, the project manager, completed the assignment well before the deadline which was quite impressive.

Suggested Answers:

1. *The research team presented us with the quite surprising results of the survey last Friday.*

2. *The young scientist from Germany travelled all the way to the annual conference, where he won an award for his innovative work.*

3. *My colleague James and I will be leading the new project approved by the board last week.*

4. *The project manager, Mary, impressively completed the assignment with her team well before the deadline.*

Stick to the Word Order Rule

Although it often causes no issues in shorter, more straight forward sentences, you should stick to this rule because the interposed phrase or clause needlessly interrupts the natural order of the main clause. This can cause confusion and miscommunication when dealing with longer, more complex sentences. In the first example above, when we read the sentence *"there's a large reservoir in the area that we need to build around,"* we cannot possibly know for certain whether the writer is saying that we need to build around the area or whether he or she is saying that we need to build around the reservoir. The second version of this sentence leaves no room for interpretation: *"We need to build around a large reservoir in the area. "*

Relative Pronouns

As a rule, the relative pronoun should come immediately after its antecedent.

Example 1:

He wrote an article about his recent project, which was published in May's newsletter.

Should read:

He published an article in May's newsletter about his recent project.

Example 2:

This is the Chicago headquarters of Push Co., which is the subsidiary of S.P. Inc. It supplies the entire state of Illinois.

Should read:

This is the Chicago headquarters of Push Co., a subsidiary of S.P. Inc., which supplies the entire state of Illinois.

Exercise:

Revise the following sentences to ensure that the relative pronoun comes immediately after its antecedent. Check your answers on the next page.

1. My brother James, is an expert in quantum physics. He teaches at a university in California.

2. We visited the old mansion just outside of town. The mansion is rumored to be haunted.

3. Alina, the owner of the gym on Clair Street, is planning an event. The event is a corporate event, and it is tomorrow night at Hotel Lexa.

Suggested Answers:

1. *My brother James, who is an expert in quantum physics, teaches at a university in California.*

2. *We visited the old mansion just outside of town, which is rumored to be haunted.*

3. *Alina, the owner of the gym on Clair Street, is planning a corporate event at Hotel Lexa tomorrow night.*

Active VS Passive

Active Voice

It's a good idea to use the active voice if possible, as it creates more organized, clear, and vivid sentences in general. Passive voice sentences are often longer and use more obscure word combinations, but they're also less specific and can lead to disconnected readers.

Examples:

Active: *Mary Higgins handles the new accounts.*

Active: *Mary Higgins is handling the new accounts.*

Active: *Mary Higgins must handle the new accounts.*

Passive Voice

The active voice usually is more straightforward and more potent than the passive:

Most of our New York office will be attending the conference. (Active)

This is clearer and more concise than:

The conference will be attended by most of our New York office. (Passive)

Using the passive when it is not necessary can sometimes produce ridiculous sentences like:

The conference will be attended by me next week.

If you try to tidy up this passive sentence by removing "*by me,*" you turn it into an indefinite:

The conference will be attended next week.

The sentence is now too unclear.

Who is going to be attending the conference?

Is it an unknown group of people?

Are we referring to people in general?

It's always better to write and say: *I will be attending the conference next week.*

Exercise

Transform the following sentences from passive voice to active voice. Check your answers on the next page.

1. The quarterly report was presented by our team leader.

2. The new marketing strategy will be implemented by our department.

3. The proposal was being reviewed by the board of directors.

Suggested Answers

1. *Our team leader presented the quarterly report.*

2. *Our department will implement the new marketing strategy.*

3. *The board of directors was reviewing the proposal.*

Using Nouns in Business Writing

Efficient writers often use nouns and noun phrases to save time and use less words.

Here is an example:

At an <u>investigative level</u> the <u>availability</u> of <u>digital resources</u>, <u>simulators</u> and <u>other tools</u> provide researchers with increased <u>access</u> to information, which they would otherwise not have.

A large portion of that sentence is made up of nouns. Using nouns can be extremely efficient, when you need to mention several things.

The above example is far more efficient than writing:

When carrying out research, having digital resources, being able to carry out simulations, and having other tools, means that researchers can access information that they would otherwise not be able to access.

Writing about processes without describing the action, is a useful way of compressing information:

Temperature increase	*Price drop*
Efficiency increase (increase in efficiency)	*Interest rate manipulation*

Note: Ideally, you should aim to have a mixture of structures to avoid repetitiveness.

Exercise

Change the sentences by using nouns instead of verbs where possible.

The trick is to find the verbs first, then transform some of them into nouns, e.g.:

The area would benefit if businesses increased the amount they produced.

The area would benefit from an increase in business productivity/ business production.

1. The local government should train their employees better so that they can be more efficient.

   ....
   ....

2. There is a difference between cultures so they need to communicate by using different strategies.

   ....
   ....

3. If governments around the world implement this strategy, they may reduce the pollution.

   ....
   ....

4. If they recycle waste, they may have a better chance of reducing poverty in the area

   ....
   ....

Exercise

Suggested Answers

1. Better employee training would increase the local government's efficiency. / With better employee training the local government's efficiency would increase.

2. Cultural differences need/require a wide range of/different communication strategies.

3. The implementation of this strategy by (world) governments may lead to reductions in pollution.

4. The recycling of waste may improve chances of reducing poverty in the area / may lead to a reduction of poverty in the area / may lead to an improved chance of reducing poverty in the area.

Diplomacy

This business English writing book prepares you for writing within a professional setting where you often need to be respectful of the ideas of others, particularly in writing. It would often look very bad if you wrote something like *'these people are completely wrong'* or *'I think these researchers were wrong'*.

Use cautious language. This is also called 'hedging' language, because 'to hedge against something' means to protect yourself from its negative consequences.

Instead, you need to express yourself in a more diplomatic way, for example: *'However, it might be the case that ....'* or *'Recent research suggests that this is not always the case.'* You are supposed to analyze different sides and project a sense of impartiality while you say whether you agree or disagree. Remember you always need to remain modest about your opinion and show the reader that you understand that you may be wrong just like anybody else.

Here are some examples:

"Graduate trainees have a very low level of basic mathematical knowledge due to over-dependence on calculators."

This is the writer's personal opinion, but she/he cannot write this without evidence.

*"Over-dependence on calculators **may** have a negative effect on the basic mathematical knowledge of **some graduate trainees**"*

Don't be too cautious

People often make the mistake of using cautious language where it is not appropriate. They sometimes use 'would', 'might', 'likely to', etc. because they have learnt that these verbs are common in professional writing.

For example: *"Annual financial reports **might** include information from financial statements and other sources."*

You don´t need to know a lot about accounting or business to know that the objective of financial reports is to provide financial information taken from financial statements and other sources. Therefore, the verb *'might'* can't be used here.

Exercise: Being Specific

Eliminate the word 'thing' in these sentences and add a more specific word or phrase.

1. The availability of water has a significant effect on every living thing.

2. This environment is made up of non-living things like air, water and rocks.

3. It is essential from a scientific perspective to investigate every single thing that is possible.

Exercise:

Suggested Answers:

1. *The availability of water has a significant effect on every living* **organism/being.**

2. *This environment is made up of non-living* **elements** *like air, water and rocks.*

3. *It is essential from a scientific perspective to investigate every single* **possibility/possible factor.**

Remember...

Link your sentences in formal writing

Always use Linking Adverbs like *therefore, additionally, consequently, firstly, secondly, finally, moreover, however*

Use synonyms to replace basic level vocabulary

To (purpose): in order to, so as to

Like = *such as, for example, for instance*

Get = *receive, acquire, obtain*

Help = *aid, assist, support*

Not only does X do Y but it also does Z

Look at the difference between these sentences....

Version 1: *Working gives you experience to help your career prospects. Working also improves important skills like social skills.*

Version 2: *Not only does working provide you with experience to help your career prospects, but it also improves essential skills such as social abilities and communication.*

Chapter 9. Writing Email & Letter References

In this type of formal email or letter, you are required to provide a reference for a colleague or friend to a prospective employer or educational institution.

You may find it helpful to note down useful expressions which you can include,

Some Useful Language for this type of letter or email

I have known X for ....

I am confident that ....

I have no hesitation in recommending her ....

X is sociable, reliable, self-confident, outgoing

X possesses a thorough grounding in ...

stand him in good stead

as is shown by the fact that …

There are four important components: content, organization, language and communicative achievement. Including all the relevant content in your letter and presenting it clearly is vital.

Here is a typical example of a formal letter. We will practice identifying key content, working through the task chronologically.

Read the example and answer the following question.

1. What is the first key piece of information you need to refer to in your answer?

A friend of yours is applying for a job in a popular shop, as a retail shop assistant for English speaking tourists visiting your city. The shop has asked you to provide a character reference for your friend. The reference should indicate how long you have known each other. It must include a detailed description of the person's character and the reason why he or she would be suitable for the job.

Write your reference. (220-260 words)

It's important to use a formal register. For example:

"To whom it may concern,

Mary and I have been working together at J&J Retail for 10 years.

…………….."

2. What is the next important information?

We need to pay attention to the type of job we are writing the reference for. The job in this case is a retail assistant for a popular shop. It is important to remember that the information we provide must be relevant for this position.

3. What qualities or skills does a suitable candidate for almost any job need to have?

You can use the following ideas for any job reference.

i. Personal and social skills (people skills/inter-personal abilities): The successful candidate will need to have good personal and social skills so, if applicable, we must emphasize the person's personal and social skills in the context of their application.

ii. Time-management ability is another skill that every person needs for a job, so regardless of the job you are presented with, you can talk about this.

4. So what's next?

Previous experience. We need to mention any relevant work the person has done in the past that will support their application. Again, we could link this with the earlier part about their people skills or about their time-management skills.

We need to show the person is suitable for the post, but this doesn't necessarily need to be in a separate paragraph. You can write about their experience in the same paragraph whilst you describe their character and skills.

Alternatively, it could be something you include at the end of the letter but either way, you always need to emphasize the person's suitability for the post.

Organization:

Read the example again and answer the following questions.

1. How many paragraphs would you have?

2. Which paragraphs would deal with which issues?

Example

A friend of yours is applying for a job in a popular shop, as a retail shop assistant for English speaking tourists visiting your city. The shop has asked you to provide a character reference for your friend. The reference should indicate how long you have known each other. It must include a detailed description of the person's character and the reason why he or she would be suitable for the job.

One idea is to organize this around two or three content paragraphs along with an opening and closing paragraph, so four or five paragraphs in total.

Paragraph 1

The first paragraph is going to deal with our reason for writing. In this case, to write a reference (or in the letter of application to apply for something). In a letter of reference or a letter of application, the first main content paragraph usually outlines the person's skills and experience, perhaps including any relevant qualifications they might have. So in this first paragraph we could answer the sections which are underlined in the question.

Paragraph 2

Then, we could move on to look at the person's character and personal qualities.

We could deal with the person's suitability for the post in these two paragraphs if we wanted to or we could choose to have a third content paragraph where we emphasize the person's strengths once again.

Finally, we would end the letter with a closing remark such as

"Please do not hesitate to contact me if you require any further information".

Organizing your paragraphs in a logical way like this would make the letter coherent overall and it would give the reader a visual guide to your organization especially if you leave a line or a space between each paragraph. It would also help you deal with the main sections of the letter in a logical order.

Expressing Ideas:

But what about how you express ideas within paragraphs? How can you link ideas in and between sentences? Let's look at some of the ways you can do this.

Linking Words:

The first method is the use of straightforward linking words that you've probably used in your writing for a while. Words or expressions like "firstly" or "in addition", or "for instance". These enable you to link ideas simply and effectively.

Discourse Markers:

These are just slightly higher-level linking words or expressions such as "moreover", "furthermore" or "by way of example".

Exercise:

Look at the gaps in the sample answer below:

Where could you use these linking words and discourse markers to complete the text? You will not need to use all of them.

Firstly, in addition, for instance, moreover, furthermore or by way of example.

Sample Answer (Character Reference):

To whom it may concern,

Jane and I worked together at J&J Media for 10 years.

It is my pleasure to recommend her for the position of media assistant at XL Media Ltd.

1......................., Jane is a self-confident and outgoing person, who finds it easy to relate to people from all kinds of backgrounds.

During her time at J&J Media, Jane proved to be friendly, communicative, hard-working and excellent at managing her time. 2......................, Jane is the kind of person who works well with others, as she displays great sensitivity and empathy. She was always willing to contribute to the team and help her colleagues. 3.................... at J&J Media, she was popular and fully committed to the organization's objectives.

Jane mentioned to me that this role at your company would involve dealing with corporate clients and I believe that she is remarkably well-suited for this task. 4.................... at J&J Media, Jane demonstrated excellent communication skills dealing with corporate clients on a daily basis. She also has a keen interest in new media, which I am sure will stand her in good stead when she is helping clients.

I recommend Jane without reservation — she would be an excellent asset to your company.

Please do not hesitate to contact me if you have any questions.

Sincerely,

Your name and Surname

Sample Answer (Reference/ Character Reference):

To whom it may concern,

Jane and I worked together at J&J Media for 10 years.

It is my pleasure to recommend her for the position of Media Assistant at your XL Media Ltd.

Firstly, Jane is a self-confident and outgoing person, who finds it easy to relate to people from all kinds of backgrounds.

During her time at J&J Media, Jane proved to be friendly, communicative, hard-working and excellent at managing her time. In addition, Jane is the kind of person who works well with others, as she displays great sensitivity and empathy. She was always willing to contribute to the team and help her colleagues. Moreover, (Furthermore) at J&J Media she was popular and fully committed to the organization's objectives.

Jane mentioned to me that this role at your company would involve dealing with corporate clients, and I believe that she is remarkably well-suited for this task. By way of example, (For instance) at J&J Media, Jane demonstrated excellent communication skills dealing with corporate clients on a daily basis. She also has a keen interest in new media, which I am sure will stand her in good stead when she is helping clients.

I recommend Jane without reservation — she would be an excellent asset to your company.

Please do not hesitate to contact me if you have any questions.

Sincerely,

Notes:

Reference pronouns:

Reference pronouns like *this, that, they* or *it* are commonly used to refer back to something or someone recently mentioned.

Relative clauses:

Relative clauses can be used to give added information to a statement and they allow you to link ideas together in well-formed sentences.

Substitution:

Other forms of cohesive devices include using substitution. This is where you use a synonym for example to refer backwards or forwards to a connected point in the text.

E.g. Replacing a verb phrase:

The management team at J & J Media were very happy with Jane, and so were the rest of the staff (and the rest of the staff were also very happy with her).

Using paragraphs and a variety of cohesive devices effectively will help you to produce a well-organized piece of writing. When you are reading other people´s writing, make a point of looking out for cohesive devices like the ones we have looked at in this section.

Chapter 10. Email Applications & Cover Letters

Introduction to Formal Letters and Emails

If you need to write a formal letter or email applying for a job or place on a course, it is very important that you get it right. Again, the recipient of this letter is a prospective employer or educational institution, so the register should always be formal and well presented.

Importance and Guidelines for Cover Letters

Cover letters, sometimes called letters of application, are a very important part of your application, whether you are a student at university or a candidate looking for a job. While there are virtually no limits to the different designs you can use for your letter of application, there are some general guidelines, which you will want to stick to, in order to make sure it is appropriate.

Creating an Excellent First Impression

It is first important to make sure your cover letter has an excellent appearance in terms of both structure and language. Make sure you learn the name of the person or organization that you are writing to if possible, and remember that the name must always be spelled correctly

.

Highlighting Your Qualifications for the Job

The next thing you want to do is to demonstrate your qualifications for the job. It is best to write two powerful sentences explaining why you have the necessary skills to perform the job you are interested in. After this, you will want to let the potential employer know that your resume is enclosed or attached. It is also important to make sure you do not end the letter incorrectly.

Imagine you see this advertisement in an international student magazine.

Volunteers needed

We are looking for volunteers to help out at a famous, international sporting event. We're looking for friendly, respectful people with good language skills, good team skills and a 'can-do' attitude. We need people to welcome delegates, provide customer service and solve problems.

If you think you have what it takes, apply now!

(Source: Exam English)

The first key piece of information you should mention in your application is the fact you've seen the advertisement and where you saw it. This will be the perfect way to start the letter.

Remember that you also need to confirm which position it is you're applying for, as there may be more than one position. If you didn't mention the specific job, the reader would not be fully informed.

For example:

Dear Sir or Madam,

I am writing to apply for the Volunteer position advertised on the Harvard Business Review website.

Language Skills or Communication Skills

In this example, the fact that the sporting event is international will give you the chance to emphasize your language skills such as your ability to speak Spanish fluently.

Communication skills are something which you can and should arguably always mention in a letter of application. All positions advertised will require the candidate to speak or write effectively.

Suitability for the job

You need to explain your suitability for the job. The question will sometimes state what the required skills or knowledge are, but normally you'll have to include your experience, your qualifications, if any, and personal qualities.

Availability for interview

Finally, it would be a good idea to point out that you're available for interview and perhaps to state any times when you're not available. If you cover all these points in your answer clearly, logically, persuasively and in an appropriate format, you will have a far greater chance of landing the interview.

Exercise

Write your answer in 220-260 words in an appropriate style.

You see this advertisement in an international student magazine.

Volunteers needed

We are looking for volunteers to help out at a famous, international sporting event. We're looking for friendly, respectful people with good language skills, good team skills and a 'can-do' attitude. We need people to welcome delegates, provide customer service and solve problems.

If you think you have what it takes, apply now!

Write an application to become a volunteer.

You should mention:

your language skills

your personal qualities

examples of times when you have demonstrated team skills

any relevant work experience

(Source: Exam English)

(Write below)

Sample Answer

Dear Mr/Mrs/Miss/Ms [Hiring managers name — "Dear Sir or Madam" if name or gender are unknown]

I wish to apply for the role of [Volunteer] advertised in the [International Student Magazine]. Please find attached my CV for your consideration.

As you can see from my attached CV, I have over [time period, eg: 5 years] experience in [eg; volunteering or customer service], and I believe the knowledge and skills built up during this time make me the perfect candidate for this position. I am also keen to keep improving my Spanish, as this is not only a hobby but also a real need.

In my current role as a [job title] at [employer name], I have been responsible for [e.g. a 5% increase in revenue], which when coupled with my enthusiasm and dedication [insert skills relevant to the role — usually found in the job description], has helped the business to [measure of success].

I am confident that I can bring this level of success with me to your organization and help [company name] build upon their reputation as an outstanding company. With my previous experience and expertise, I believe my contribution will have an immediate impact on the business.

Thank you for your time and consideration.

I look forward to meeting with you to discuss my application further.

Yours sincerely/ Yours faithfully,

[Your name]

Chapter 11. Writing Formal Complaints

Up until now, we have concentrated on identifying the key content, which is the most important information we need to provide in our communication. We need to provide ALL the key content if we want it to have a positive impact on the reader.

Good organization is about using logical paragraphs, as well as clear organization of ideas. You do this by using linking words, discourse markers and other devices. The examples in the previous section show you exactly how to organize your letter of reference and letter of application but they do not show you how to organize other types of letter.

In this section, we are going to practice use of language and features of organization, as they are crucial when defending your ideas.

Exercise:

Example:

0) Basic Problem: *"I want to complain about the bad service in the restaurant. "*

ii. Key Language: *I would like to express my dissatisfaction with ...*

iii, Key Word you must use: POOR (Bad is too informal, so we can use *poor* instead)

iv. Final Product: *"I would like to express my dissatisfaction with the poor standard of service in the restaurant. "*

Now try to complete the process using the following language:

1)

i. Basic problem: *"The cinema is really far away from everything"*

ii. Key Phrase: *I wish to complain in the strongest terms about...*

iii, Key Word: ACCESSIBILITY

iv. Final Product:

....
....
....

2)

i. Basic problem: *"During my course, there were too many students in the class"*

ii. Key Phrase: *I am writing to express my concern about the....*

iii, Key Word: NUMBER

iv. Final Product:

....
....
....

Answers:

1) I wish to complain in the strongest terms about the accessibility of the cinema.

2) I am writing to express my concern about the number of students in the class during my course

Organization

Read this extract from a message you have recently sent to a work friend:

".... I forgot to say, don't go to Dino's Bar for the meeting. We went there last night - the service was awful, the food was cold and it was so expensive for such a bad meal! I complained to a member of staff but she asked me to put it in writing ..."

How would you organize an email of complaint in this situation?

There are several ways to approach this letter, but one suggestion is to organize it around four content paragraphs, one for each problem and one at the end for suggestions.

The letter or email can be planned and organized as follows:

4 paragraphs:

1. Formal "hello" and state general problem, saying why you went to Dino´s in this case and that you are dissatisfied. State problem 1 (the service was awful)

2. Detailed explanation of problem 2 (the food was cold)

3. Problem 3: the price was expensive

4. Conclusion, what you want Dino´s to do- offer some suggestions here for improvement here.

A bit more on each paragraph:

The first paragraph deals with your reason for writing. In a written complaint, the first main content paragraph is used to:

- Outline the problem
- Say why you went to the business you are complaining about
- Make sure you clearly state that you are dissatisfied.

In the second paragraph, we could look at the specific details of the problem, using appropriate adjectives.

Finally, in the last paragraph, we could offer some suggestions or recommendations to help the business improve in the future. You can use language such as:

I must insist that you...

I urge you to...

Exercise

Re-read this extract from a message you have recently sent to a work friend:

".... I forgot to say, don't go to Dino's Bar for the meeting. We went there last night - the service was awful, the food was cold and it was so expensive for such a bad meal! I complained to a member of staff but she asked me to put it in writing ..."

Using the information appropriately, write your complaint to the manager of Dino's bar (around 220-260 words). There is a sample email on the next page:

(Answer Below)

Now look at the sample answer for the question we looked at earlier in this section. Pay special attention to the language and structure used.

Task

Read this extract from a letter you have recently sent to a friend:

".... I forgot to say, don't go to Dino's Bar for your meeting. We went there last night - the service was awful, the food was cold and it was so expensive for such a bad meal! I complained to a member of staff but he asked me to put it in writing ..."

Using the information appropriately, write your letter of complaint to the manager of Dino´s bar (around 220-260 words)

<u>Sample Answer</u>

Dear Sir/ Madam,

I would like to express my dissatisfaction with the poor standard of service we received during our recent visit to Dino´s Bar.

Firstly, the staff were generally quite rude and unhelpful, they seemed to lack basic food knowledge and they did not seem interested in the job. For instance, none of them could offer any advice to me on choosing a dish.

A further cause for complaint was that the food was cold when it arrived to our table. I understand that it was a busy night, but, we booked the table and the menus the day before, so I feel that they should have been ready.

Finally, not only did we receive substandard food and unfriendly, unhelpful service, but we were also charged full price for our meals after we complained. In my opinion the prices seem to be very expensive for the quality of the food and the service provided.

I do not usually complain, but, as a loyal customer, I hope you will be interested in my comments. Perhaps it would be appropriate to offer some training courses to staff at

Dino's Bar, in order to avoid this from happening again. I feel that customer service was a big issue, as was the quality of the food. If these two problems were fixed, then price might not be such an issue in the future, as customers would be happy to pay little more for a better experience. I hope you will take these points into consideration

I look forward to your reply.

Yours faithfully,

Name and Surname

Written Complaint Phrase Bank

I am writing to complain about...

I would like to express my dissatisfaction with ...

I am writing to express my concern about the....

I must complain in writing about...

I feel I must complain to you about...

I wish to complain in the strongest terms about...

I am writing to inform you of an apparent error in your records...

Topic specific phrases

- *Poor standard of service/ slow service*

- *I am asking for/ I would like to request a replacement*

- *No accommodation/ Travel delays/ Rather rude staff*

- *Badly scratched/ dented wrapping/ packaging*

- *To claim/ demand for a refund*

- *I am returning ... to you for correction of the fault/ for inspection/ repair/ servicing*

- *Defective/ faulty goods/ defective item/ machine*

- *The... may need replacing*

- *To restore an item to full working order...*

- *I am enclosing the broken radio in this package; please send me a replacement..*

- *You said that ... I feel sure there must be some mistake as I am sure that...*

Ending the letter

- *I do not usually complain, but, as an old customer, I hope you will be interested in my comments.*

- *We look forward to dealing with this matter without delay.*

- *I feel that yo ur company should consider an appropriate refund.*

- *I would be grateful if you would send me a complete refund as soon as possible*

- *We feel there must be some explanation for (this delay) and expect your prompt reply.*

- *Will you please look into this matter and let us know the reason for ...*

- *Thank you for your assistance.*

- *I look forward to hearing from you at your earliest convenience.*

- *I am returning the damaged goods/items… and shall be glad if you will replace them.*

- *Please look into this matter at once and let me know the delay.*

- *Please check your records again.*

- *Thank you for your cooperation in correcting this detail…*

- *I wish to draw your attention to…*

- *I would suggest that…*

- *I suggest that immediate steps be taken.*

- *I wish to complain about…*

- *I look forward to a prompt reply and hope that you will take into consideration…*

- *I am really dissatisfied with…*

Formal Letter: Structure Rules

Greeting

Name unknown: *Dear Sir/Madam,*

Name known: *Dear Mr…/ Dear Mrs… / Dear Ms..+ surname*

Reason for writing

I am writing to … I am writing with regard to …

I am writing on behalf of …

Asking questions

I would be grateful if ...   *I wonder if you could ....*

Could you ...?

Referring to someone else´s letter /points

As you stated in your letter, ... Regarding .../ Concerning ...

With regard to ....

Finishing the letter

If you require any further information, please do not hesitate to contact me.

I look forward to hearing from you.

Signing

If Dear + name = Yours sincerely,

If Dear Sir/ Madam = Yours faithfully

Your first name + surname must be written clearly under your signature

Chapter 12. Formal English Language Review

In this chapter, we will focus on language use and in particular, your ability to create a formal register. We will identify some of the features of formal English that we often find in formal emails and letters.

At the end of this section you will find a list of useful formal-informal equivalents. This list will hopefully save you a lot of time in your writing.

Exercise 1:

Transform the informal or semi-formal version of each phrase from a letter of complaint into a formal style. You can make small changes to the content of the sentences if you think it's necessary and you can use a dictionary.

Example: I thought I'd write = I am writing

a. state of the playground =

b. I have noticed loads of rubbish =

c. I reckon =

d. The teacher I'm talking about =

e. On top of this =

f. a load of problems =

g. You could =

h. stop =

i. What's more =

j. better =

k. To finish =

l. I'm looking forward to hearing from you =

Suggested Answers:

a. state of the playground = condition of the playground

b. I have noticed loads of rubbish = There is a great deal of litter

c. I reckon = It is my opinion that…

d. The teacher I'm talking about = The teacher in question OR The teacher I am referring to

e. On top of this = Furthermore

f. a load of problems = a number of problems

g. You could = it may be possible for you

h. stop = prevent

i. What's more = In addition

j. better = more suitable OR more adequate

k. To finish = In conclusion

l. I'm looking forward to hearing from you = I look forward to your reply OR I look forward to hearing from you

Exercise 2:

Now here are some full sentences from formal letters. Complete the sentences using only one word.

a. I am writing in .... to your job advertisement in the ABC newspaper

b. I would like to .... for the position of translator.

c. I am .... to come for interview at any time convenient to you.

d. I would be .... if you could send me further information regarding the position.

e. Please find my CV ....

f. I would like to express my .... with the poor standard of service we received during our recent visit to your cinema.

g. For ...., none of them could offer any advice to me on choosing a dish.

h. Finally, not only .... we receive substandard food and unfriendly, unhelpful service, but we were also charged full price for our meals after we complained.

i. I look forward to your reply.

Answers:

a. I am writing in reply/response to your job advertisement in the ABC newspaper

b. I would like to apply for the position of translator.

c. I am available/ able to come for interview at any time convenient to you.

d. I would be grateful if you could send me further information regarding the position.

e. Please find my CV attached (email)/ enclosed (letter).

f. I would like to express my dissatisfaction with the poor standard of service we received during our recent visit to your cinema.

g. For instance, none of them could offer any advice to me on choosing a dish.

h. Finally, not only did we receive substandard food and unfriendly, unhelpful service, but we were also charged full price for our meals after we complained.

i. I look forward to your reply.

Use of the Passive in Formal Writing

The next example is one where the passive has been used instead of an active form. This is a common feature of formal writing but should not be overused.

This sentence is an example of how we might structure a sentence formally.

Informal: *"The waiter did offer us another dish, but when it arrived it was cold again."*

Formal: *"Although we were offered an alternative dish, when it was delivered to the table it was once again cold".*

Notice two clauses in the informal version are joined by *but* whereas in the formal version, the two clauses have been reversed and *but* is replaced with *although* which starts the sentence. This is a more formal way of saying the same thing.

Within the formal sentence *"Although we were offered an alternative dish, when it was delivered to the table it was once again cold".* there are further examples of vocabulary that is more formal than the equivalent in the informal version. For example, *alternative dish* is a more formal way of saying *another dish.*

Quick Rules for Formal VS Informal Writing

1. We tend to understate our feelings and would say *I was rather disappointed* or *I was somewhat surprised* instead of saying how we really felt.

2. For the same reason, we do not use exclamation marks.

3. We often use the passive to emphasize the action when the person is of less importance

4. We avoid contractions in formal letters and emails.

5. We use formal equivalence of idiomatic language and phrasal verbs

6. Particular sentence structures can be used to create a formal tone. Inversion is one example of this "*Although we were offered an alternative dish, when it was delivered to the table it was cold again*".

Exercise 3:

Rewrite the following sentences using formal equivalents for the phrasal verbs. Use a dictionary if necessary. You might need to make other changes to the structures.

1) I'm so chuffed that you've been talked into coming to the meeting.

....
....

....
....

2) The football club's facilities have been done up, so this should make our performances better.

....
....

....
....

3) As our town is quite cut off, perhaps we could arrange for you to be put up in a hotel in the city for a few days.

....
....

....
....

4) We will make up for the inconvenience of having to wait for so long.

....
....

Answers:

1) I am very happy that you have been convinced to attend the meeting.

2) The football club's facilities have been refurbished, which should improve our performances.

3) As our town is quite isolated, we could arrange hotel accommodation in the city for a few days.

4) We will compensate you for the inconvenience of having to wait for so long.

Chapter 13. Better Email Memos

Short- Focused

Email memos tend to be concise. They normally aim to give the reader an overall understanding of an issue without the formalities of a full report.

To keep things short and effective, try to follow the "no scrolling" or "one screen" rule, which dictates that all the information your reader needs can be found on the first screen of the message without them having to scroll down. You can do this by placing the most important information at the beginning of the message.

Subject Line

The subject line is an important part of the e-mail memo as it gives the reader an idea of your message and allows them to decide whether or not to open it. To make the most of the subject line, include key information, such as the answer to the question being addressed (if applicable). This saves your reader time and effort.

Here are some examples of e-mail memo subject lines:

"Response to Inquiry about Information Privacy Policies"

"Recommended Approach for Negotiating Contractual Differences"

"Progress Report on X Project Application"

"Assessment of Accountability for Recent Operational Incident"

"Final Analysis on X Business Agreement Feasibility"

Writing Email Memos

Main Question:

When beginning the body of the e-mail memo, it's important to restate the question being asked or the main topic of the memo. This helps to ensure that the reader has a clear understanding of the issue.

Use basic language:

"Dear Jack, you needed me to research blah blah blah..."

Briefly respond:

Before analyzing, answer the question briefly. Most supervisors or clients need answers upfront. One to three sentences are usually enough.

This can be done in a single paragraph or using bullet points. It's important to be thorough in your answer and to provide reasons for your conclusion, as this explains your reasoning and makes your argument easier to follow.

Finally, conclude the e-mail memo by outlining any important next steps or recommendations. This could involve suggesting a course of action or providing further information that might be useful to the reader. Again, it's important to be clear and concise in your recommendations and ensure they're relevant to the issue being addressed.

If you are unsure, writing case explanations for your understanding may be helpful. However, including these explanations in the e-mail memo is generally unnecessary. They can clutter the text and make it more challenging to read.

For example:

Let's say the question is: *"Should our company invest in online advertising?"*

Brief Response:

Yes, our company should definitely invest in online advertising. The benefits include increased visibility, targeted marketing, and measurable results.

Analysis:

- *Increased Visibility: With more people spending time online, online advertising would significantly increase our brand's exposure and reach a wider audience.*

- *Targeted Marketing: Online advertising allows us to target specific demographics based on their interests, behaviors, and other factors. This can lead to more effective and efficient marketing.*

- *Measurable Results: Online advertising platforms provide detailed analytics. We can track our ads' performance and adjust our strategies based on real-time data.*

In conclusion, investing in online advertising can provide significant benefits and is aligned with current market trends. This step could be pivotal in boosting our growth.

Offer extra assistance:

Supervisors and clients may ask follow-up questions. Ending your email with *"Please do not hesitate to get back to me with any questions"* shows your work ethic and sets the tone for a fruitful relationship.

Template 1: Copyright Email Memo

TO: [   ]

FROM: [   ]

DATE: [   ]

SUBJECT: Copyright Infringement on Vimeo

Dear [Name],

Your request for information regarding the uploading of full movie content on Vimeo by a big media label, which is under the authority of XYZ Ltd, has been received. It has been noted that the videos have not yet been removed by the management team.

Under the Fair Use Copyright Act of 1974, it is possible to use copyrighted material without permission in certain circumstances, such as criticism, commentary, news reporting, teaching, scholarship, or research. However, if the unauthorized use does not meet the criteria for fair use, Vimeo must file a copyright claim and send a takedown notice to the responsible company.

The parties' involvement has been submitted for review and is being carefully discussed to avoid errors in decision-making. Please see the attached file for further information.

Thank you.

Template 2: Explaining Rules: Interoffice Memo

INTEROFFICE MEMO

TO: [   ]

FROM: [   ]

DATE: [   ]

SUBJECT: **Purchasing [Safety Goggles]**

Dear [Name],

Safety goggles are required for all employees at all times in areas near machinery is being operated. These areas are:

X

Y

Z

All employees who are required to wear safety goggles are reimbursed following 15 days of employment.

Safety goggle specifications:

- *Safety glasses should be made of polycarbonate*

- *Lens should be 3mm thick*

- *Lens should be scratch-resistant*

- *Lens should be fog-free*

- *Safety glasses should have side shields for added protection*

The procedure for purchasing safety goggles is as follows:

- *Obtain Safety Goggle Authorization Form from HR Department.*

- *Refer to the form for a list of authorized stores.*

- *Purchase goggles from one of the designated stores and keep the receipt.*

- *Fill out the form and attach the receipt.*

- *Return the receipt and Safety Goggle Authorization Form to Human Resources Department.*

- *After 15 days, HR will issue a transfer to your designated bank account for the price specified in the receipt for the goggles.*

- *Employees are entitled to 1 new pair of safety goggles each year.*

If you have any questions or concerns, please contact Mary Higgins from Human Resources: mary.higgins@xyzlawfirm.com. Tel: 555 555 555.

Kind regards,

[Your Name]

Template 3: Reprimanding: Interoffice Memo

TO: [   ]

FROM: [   ]

DATE: [   ]

SUBJECT: Not following established procedures

ABC Ltd. has an established quality control procedure (ref.1023) for calculating the levels of sodium nitrate in bottled drinking water produced in all its plants. The procedure involves analyzing ten samples of filled bottles, 10 minutes apart from each production line, and measuring the amount of sodium nitrate in the water.

On June 10 and July 7, the team on the 7 am-12 pm shift failed to follow the standard procedure. On June 10, only one sample was taken from each of the three production lines that were in operation. The amount of sodium nitrate was subsequently found to be above 10 milligrams per liter of drinking water (mg/L). The U.S. Environmental Protection Agency (EPA) standard for nitrate in drinking water is 10 milligrams of nitrate (measured as nitrogen) per liter of drinking water (mg/L).

The employees on the production line at the time were

Jim Jones

Trevor Edmunds

Tracey Stimpson

Jerry Sanchez

Morty McFly

We have initiated a full investigation into how this was allowed to happen on two separate occasions. The results of this investigation will be carefully considered before any decisions are made regarding disciplinary action.

We are committed to maintaining the highest standards of quality in our products, and we appreciate your cooperation and understanding as we work to resolve this matter. Please do not hesitate to reach out if you have any questions or concerns.

Re-cap:

- Consider the preferences of your audience when writing an e-mail memo

- Keep the length of the e-mail memo as short as possible

- Use the subject line to provide key information

- Restate the question being asked in the body of the message

- Provide the answer with reasons in a single paragraph or bullet points

- Include analysis as needed to support your answer

- Conclude with any important next steps or recommendations

- Be concise and clear in your writing

- If you are not sure, writing case explanations for your own understanding may be helpful, but avoid including them in the e-mail memo.

Chapter 14. Setting Healthy Email Boundaries with Colleagues & Clients

Introduction

Setting boundaries with colleagues, suppliers, and clients is essential to maintaining a healthy and productive work environment. Boundaries help establish expectations and ensure everyone is treated with respect and professionalism. By setting boundaries, we communicate our needs and respect the needs of others, leading to better relationships and a more positive work experience.

Action Steps

- Communicate your expectations and availability to your colleagues and clients. This can include setting office hours, establishing a preferred method of communication, and outlining your role and responsibilities on a project.

- Consistently enforce your boundaries. If a colleague or client crosses a boundary, address the issue directly and firmly. This helps to establish that your limits are to be respected.

- Be firm but fair when dealing with clients. If a client requests something outside your scope of practice or expertise, it's okay to say no.

- Take care of yourself and prioritize your well-being. Setting boundaries can be challenging, but it's important to remember that it maintains a healthy work-life balance and protects your mental and physical health.

Exercise

1. Use the Record Sheet on the next page.

2. Choose ONE or TWO specific boundaries you would like to set with your colleagues, such as office hours or a preferred method of communication.

3. Communicate your boundaries to your colleagues using the action steps outlined above.

4. Observe your interactions and track instances where a boundary is crossed or respected.

5. After a set period, such as a week or a month, evaluate the effectiveness of the action steps by analyzing the data collected and assessing whether the boundaries set were consistently enforced and respected.

6. If necessary, make any adjustments to the action steps and repeat the test to continue improving the effectiveness of the boundaries you set.

Record Sheet: Establishing & Maintaining Boundaries

Name: _____

Date: _____

Boundary: _____

Colleague/Client: _____

Boundary Crossed (Yes/No): _____

Date of Incident: _____

Notes: _____

Boundary: _____

Colleague/Client: _____

Boundary Crossed (Yes/No): _____

Date of Incident: _____

Notes: _____

Availability

Setting boundaries around your availability can be challenging, especially if you're trying to build your business or practice. However, it's important to prioritize your well-being and ensure you have time to rest and recharge. By setting boundaries and communicating them, you can maintain a healthy work-life balance and build long-term success.

The following email template is provided as an example only. It should be adapted to meet the specific needs of your situation. It's important to carefully consider your circumstances before taking any action.

Example: Setting Limits

Dear [Client],

I hope this email finds you well. I wanted to reach out to discuss my availability as your X.

As you may know, I am committed to providing high-quality XYZ to all my clients. To do so, I must manage my time effectively and prioritize my workload.

With that in mind, I am available to discuss your case and provide XYZ during the following hours: [Insert specific hours].

If you need to reach me outside of these hours, please do not hesitate to call the emergency line provided in my office's voicemail. This line is for urgent matters only and should not be used for routine inquiries.

I understand that issues with X can be stressful and that you may have questions or concerns at any time. Please know that I am here to support you and will do my best to accommodate your needs within the boundaries of my availability.

Thank you for your understanding, and I look forward to continuing to work with you on your project.

Sincerely,

Scope of Work

It's essential to clearly define the scope of work with clients, colleagues, and suppliers, including any limits on the types of tasks or services you're willing to provide. This can help prevent misunderstandings and ensure that you and others have realistic expectations.

Defining the scope of work can include identifying the specific tasks or services you will provide and any limitations or exclusions. For example, you may want to specify that you will not offer advice on specific areas, or that certain tasks will need to be handed to someone else.

Setting clear boundaries around the scope of work can help you manage your workload and ensure that you can provide a high-quality service. Communicating the scope of work to your clients upfront helps set realistic expectations and avoid conflicts or misunderstandings down the road.

Example: Scope of Work

Dear [Client],

I hope this email finds you well. As we move forward with our working relationship, I wanted to take a moment to clarify the scope of our work together.

As you may recall, when we first discussed our project, we agreed that my firm would be responsible for [list specific tasks or services that have been agreed upon]. As we have begun working together, additional tasks or requests have come up that fall outside of the scope of our original agreement.

While I am happy to assist you with any needs that may arise, it is essential for both of us to have a clear understanding of the scope of our work. This includes ensuring that any additional tasks or requests are adequately documented and that any necessary adjustments to our agreement are made.

If you have any questions or concerns about the scope of our work, please don't hesitate to reach out.

Kind regards,

[Your Name]

Payment & Billing

Setting boundaries around payment and billing can include establishing policies for payment terms, late fees, and cancellations. It's also important to be clear about your rates and any additional fees or charges that may be incurred.

Using the passive voice can be useful for communicating sensitive or controversial information diplomatically and professionally. By focusing on the action or event rather than the subject performing the action, the passive voice can minimize blame or confrontation and allow the emphasis to be placed on the message itself.

Again, the following email is an example only, and you must adapt it to meet the specific needs of your situation. It's important to carefully consider your own circumstances before taking any action.

Example: Payment & Billing

SUBJECT LINE: Payment and Billing for Legal Services [Insert Relevant Dates Here]

Dear [Client],

I hope this email finds you well. I wanted to reach out regarding payment and billing for our services.

As you know, we have been category design consultation for project X on a [hourly/flat fee] basis. To ensure that our working relationship is as smooth and efficient as possible, it would be helpful to establish clear guidelines around payment and billing.

First and foremost, all time spent working on your case, including meetings, research, document drafting, and other tasks related to your project, will be billed at [insert rates] per hour (if applicable).

Out-of-pocket expenses incurred on your behalf, such as market research or the cost of materials, will also be charged. These charges, which will be itemized on your invoices, are due upon receipt.

To ensure timely payment, all payments should be made within [insert number] days of receiving an invoice.

Please let me know if you anticipate any issues with making a payment within this timeframe. We can always discuss alternative arrangements to ensure that your fees are manageable.

Thank you for your cooperation and understanding.

Passive VS Active Voice

Notice how some paragraphs have been expressed using the passive voice. This is to avoid making it too personal.

Note the difference if we wrote them in the active voice.

For example:

ACTIVE: First and foremost, we will bill you at [insert rates] per hour for all time spent working on your project, including meetings, research, document drafting, and other tasks related to the project.

VS.

PASSIVE: First and foremost, all time spent working on your case, including meetings, research, document drafting, and other tasks related to the project, will be billed at [insert rates] per hour.

Chapter 15: Better Business Reports

Introduction to Reports

This section introduces reports and looks at coming up with relevant ideas.

Reports can be very short or very long, depending on the context and on the objective. In some cases, you may be required to present data and in other cases you may be required to discuss your progress in a job or project. As we'll see, the style for this type of writing is very much towards the formal end of the spectrum.

In the later sections, we'll focus on organizing reports and we'll look at using formal language in this type of writing.

Here is an example exercise to practice your report writing skills:

You have just completed six months in a new job in preparation for a progress meeting. You have been asked to write a report to your manager. Your report should explain what you feel you've achieved in the job so far, describe any problems you've had and suggest any future training that would be suitable.

We need to break the task down into its individual components.

You've just completed six months in your new job and as is often the case at work, you have a progress meeting coming up with your manager. This of course is talking about your progress during the 6-month period at the company.

Key point: your manager has asked you to write a report for him or her to read before the meeting. You are writing to your boss so unless you are on very friendly terms, you are going to need to be formal. That is both because of the issue of seniority, he or she is higher in the organization than you, and also because a report is a formal document and it is written in a formal tone.

1. You need to explain what you think you've achieved in your first six months

2. Then, any problems you faced

3. And finally, any training needs you have.

Spend a minute or two trying to come up with ideas for this report. Drawing from your past experiences and thinking in terms of real issues will give your report a sense of authenticity.

Please Note:

- Don't fall into the trap of writing for the sake of writing.
- You need to be short and to the point to be effective.

What could you have achieved in our first six months? … imagine yourself in this situation. Think generally first, rather than in terms of specific things. Imagine you´re in a new job, what do you want to achieve in your first 6 months at the company?

Opening section

- You've probably been working in a team and you could probably mention something about fitting in well with your colleagues.
- Hopefully, you're very clear now on your roles and your responsibilities within the company.
- Perhaps, you've taken on this post following on from somebody else who has left, so maybe you've managed a smooth transition from the previous post holder.

These are just three ideas that you could use for the opening section.

Problems (Challenges)

- Think about what kind of problems you might have had. We don't have much space so you probably only need two ideas.
- You need the report to be clear; to have some sense of logic and order.
- It would be a good idea to link certain things like problems with training opportunities.
- Consider how you can solve these problems through learning and training.

Linking Challenges and Roadblocks to Training Opportunities

Having listed our challenges over the past six months the final section is relatively easy.

If you're currently working, maybe you have a specific issue in mind, but one idea is to talk about technology. Most medium and large companies are heavily reliant on technology.

- Perhaps there is some office software you found difficult to use?
- Maybe the company management information system is a bit of a mystery to you? You get the idea.

If you want a non-technology idea, then perhaps the company deals with the general public or with corporate clients and you'd like help with how to deal with highly stressed and/or angry clients. There are many possibilities.

Achievements

It would be nice to start the paragraph on a positive note, and we have three ideas to include in this paragraph. So let's have a look at an example.

Here's a nice opening sentence which summarizes the fact that things have been going well.

In general, I believe I've made a positive start to my role with the company.

We then go on to give our three examples.

I've quickly fitted into the team and have been working effectively with my colleagues. I have acquired a clear understanding of my responsibilities within the department and the wider organization, and feedback from colleagues suggests I've managed a smooth transition from the previous post holder.

It´s important to use a wide range of synonyms to keep your writing effective. Instead of repeating *company*, we use *organization,* and to avoid repeating *team*, we use *colleagues, department and members of staff*. This is going to make a much better impression than if we repeat the same words over and over.

Difficulties

Here's a sample paragraph.

Difficulties.

My role requires that I make frequent use of Microsoft PowerPoint as well as MS Excel. I feel I would be able to work more efficiently if I had a greater understanding of the potential that these software packages offer. Additionally, I'm responsible for taking phone calls from members of the public and have occasionally had difficulties dealing with complaints.

Remember that this is a formal report and you should therefore avoid informal vocabulary. We use 'my role requires that' instead of 'in my job I have to'. 'A greater understanding' is more formal than 'learn about' and of course, 'additionally' is a more formal way of saying 'also'.

We are going to look at formal language in more detail in the next section.

Opportunities for Training

Now let's turn to training. It would be useful to divide this between in-house or in-company training and training that we could access externally.

So in the example, we link this paragraph with the one before by starting with..

Bearing in mind these particular issues.

We then go on to write

I have spoken with the Human Resources team regarding training. I understand the company runs in-house workshops on using the Excel and PowerPoint which I think I would greatly benefit from.

Tip: Don´t be too friendly!

One of the key things to remember is that the report is usually for your manager, as in the example we used in the previous section. In real life, some people might have a very friendly relationship with their manager, and they might feel quite comfortable writing in an informal style, but as a general rule, it's probably best to use a semi-formal tone, since you don´t know who else might read your report.

Chapter 16: Better Business Proposals

Proposals can vary greatly in length - they can be as brief as one to two pages or as extensive as hundreds, even thousands of pages. A proposal outlines future action plans. Key features your proposal should include are:

• Clear headings for enhanced comprehension.

• A formal and impersonal style.

• Recommendations for future actions.

Tip: You don't have to write in prose like an essay. You can write in bullets to make the proposal look more professional and to help the reader understand the main points quickly.

Introduction:

Your headings should be clear, like the heading above (Introduction).

Your language should be impersonal and professional. You can use the following kind of language for your introduction:

"The aim of this proposal is to..."

"This proposal is intended to highlight the current problems with (subject of proposal) and give ideas to improve the..."

The above sentences will start out your proposal perfectly.

Current Situation:

Your next heading should explain the current situation. You will explain what the current scenario of the issue is for which you're writing a proposal.

For current situation, you can use the following type of phrases in your answer:

"As the council/company/management team/board of directors etc.. may be aware, there are issues with..."

"Following a survey among..."

"A number of concerns with regard to (some issue) were expressed by..."

Suggestions:

You should focus the major part of your proposal on future recommendations and suggestions.

You can use the following phrases when writing suggestions:

"It is suggested/recommended that..."

"(Your solution) should be created and made available to..."

Final Recommendations:

Move on to the last section of the proposal - the conclusion or the final recommendations.

Use conditional sentences for final recommendations:

"If these recommendations are implemented, the current situation with (Subject issue) will definitely improve / is bound to improve."

STEP-BY-STEP EXAMPLE

Here is a simple, fictitious example of a proposal to improve a high school.

Proposal to Improve Burnage High School

This proposal is intended to highlight the current problems with Burnage High School. It is an integral part of our community and its deterioration in recent years has affected the quality of life of local residents in the area.

Current Situation of Burnage High School:

As the council may be aware, there are issues with the state of the facilities at the high school. Following a survey among teachers and students, it was found that 85% of people interviewed believed the facilities were run-down and in some cases even dangerous. A number of concerns with regard to the sport facilities were expressed by members of staff who thought that the school should offer a wider range of activities to motivate students to lead healthier lives.

Suggestions:

It is suggested that the current school budget is more evenly distributed in order to improve parts of the school, which have been overlooked until now.

A new outside area should be created and made available to students. Furthermore, organized sporting events should be held regularly and promoted, so as to achieve greater involvement and sense of community among students.

Final Recommendations:

If these recommendations are implemented, the current situation at Burnage High School will improve / is bound to improve. I believe that modernizing the premises is the best choice and strongly urge you to consider it.

Thank You

Dear Reader,

Thank you sincerely for investing your valuable time and energy into reading this book. Your support is deeply appreciated, and I hope you found the content informative.

I am excited to offer you some additional bonus content available exclusively on our website, www.macsonbell.com This complimentary material is designed to enrich your knowledge and provide further insights beyond what has been covered in the book.

Thank you once again for joining me on this journey. I hope the concepts and ideas discussed have sparked your interest, and I look forward to continuing our journey of learning and growth together.

P.S. Your feedback and reviews are vital to helping this book reach more people. If you found the book helpful, I kindly invite you to share your thoughts and experiences by leaving a review. Your insights not only help other readers decide if this book is right for them, but also provide me with invaluable guidance to improve and refine my future work.

Warm regards,

Marc

Books in This Series

BUSINESS COMMUNICATION IN PLAIN ENGLISH

HOW TO USE GRAMMAR, PUNCTUATION & STYLE TO WRITE EFFECTIVELY IN BUSINESS AND PROFESSIONAL SETTINGS

MARC ROCHE & IDM BUSINESS ENGLISH

450 Business Writing Templates

Sign up to the **<u>FREE VIP</u>** List today, to grab your **downloadable business email and letter templates**, as well as a MS Word booklet with **425 legal documents for business**, and **MANY MORE resources** for you to use or edit as you please ☺

You will also receive a **FREE Business English Communication course** via email, with exercises and extra resources!

I hope you have found this book useful. Thank you for reading.

www.macsonbell.com/free-toolbox-sign-up-form

About the Author

MARC ROCHE is a Business Writing Coach, Legal Communication Trainer, best-selling author, and the founder of Macson Bell Training.

He has worked with organizations such as the British Council, the Royal Melbourne Institute of Technology and University of Technology Sydney, among others. Marc has also collaborated with multinationals such as Nike, GlaxoSmithKline and Bolsas y Mercados.

Marc is originally from Manchester, England..

Marc studied Business Management & Business Law at university, before gaining his teaching qualification.

In his free time, he likes to travel, cook, write, play sports, watch football (Manchester City) and spend time with friends and family.

Learn more about Marc at amazon.com/author/marcroche

FREE training resources for students and teachers

https://www.macsonbell.com/free-toolbox-sign-up-form

Made in United States
Orlando, FL
14 January 2024

42494730R00129